THE RELAXATION PRINCIPLE

This book is available at special quantity discounts for bulk purchases for sales promotions, premiums, fund raising or educational use. For details write Joy Publishing Co., 535 Cordova Rd., Santa Fe, NM 87501.

THE RELAXATION PRINCIPLE

Freedom Through a Change in Viewpoint

William F. McLaughlin

Joy Publishing Company • Santa Fe

Library of Congress Catalog
Card Number: 87-82451

ISBN: 0-9619540-0-0

First Edition

Printed in the United States of America

*"You don't have to have a brain;
you just have to know the road."*

- Scarecrow,
The Wizard of Oz

CONTENTS

PART TWO: The Process of Becoming Mentally Free

PART THREE: The Practice of Being Mentally Aware

INTRODUCTION: THE PROBLEM AND THE REMEDY

Whether or not your life works depends on how clearly you see things, and how clearly you see things depends on how relaxed you are. When relaxed, you know what you're doing, and you only do what you know. Things then fall into place for you without stress or strain, and good fortune follows as a matter of course. But when you are disturbed or excited because of something painful *or* pleasurable, the opposite becomes the case: you lose your objectivity and *think* you know what you're doing rather than *know* you know. Everything then becomes an effort and a struggle; things don't click as they should; and you experience disappointment or unfulfillment as a result.

The distinction between knowing what you're doing and thinking you know is an extremely subtle one, but makes the whole difference between frustration and success in everything you do.

Let me briefly explain, not only how excitement or disturbance affects our ability to see clearly, but also how it sets off a chain reaction process by which the problem is perpetuated indefinitely, and *without our even being aware of it.*

INTRODUCTION: THE PROBLEM AND THE REMEDY

Have you ever been so sure of something only to find you were totally wrong about it? Wasn't it bewildering? Maybe it was a school, work, or business decision or idea, or the choosing of an investment or a marriage partner, you had considered everything so carefully; you had no doubt that it was right, that it would work - then it crashed and you wondered what went wrong.

This is what happened: instead of basing your decision on matters relating to the issue itself, you got excitedly or tensely involved in it. Such involvement affected your ability to remain impartial. Instead of considering all sides of the situation dispassionately in order to make a fair judgment - you influenced it. *You took it personally instead of objectively.* Your "personal" involvement contaminated the decision-making process. Your decision wasn't based on fact, but on the influential sway of your own personality. You colored the decision. You interfered with it. You unconsciously manipulated it to coincide with how you perhaps would've *liked* it to be, or how you believed it *should* be. In other words, the decision was a biased one, causing the outcome to be inevitably different than the way you had envisioned it - different meaning negative, and negative meaning tension.

The problem is perpetuated when we carry the residual tension from past situations into the present one, insuring that it too will result negatively. On a short-term basis, it's like a person being upset over a flat tire and reacting by kicking it and stubbing his toe. Then in an angry reaction to stubbing his toe, he punches the fender and fractures his hand, and in reaction to fracturing his hand, he begins to scream obscenities, is arrested for disorderly conduct, put in a straightjacket and placed under thirty days observation, and so on.

Or more commonly, it's like being resentful over a poor golf stroke, and carrying that resentment over to negatively affect the next stroke and then the next, until your whole game is off which would cause your whole day to be off. And if we carry this cause and effect cycle on to its logical conclusion, your whole week would be off, your whole month would be off and your whole life would be off!

Other examples would be fear of dogs because of being bitten as a child, fear of starting a new business venture because of a past failure, fear of closeness or openness in a relationship because of a past hurt, and so on.

Thus are we involved in a three-way chain reaction process or vicious circle where: one, being tense causes us to not see clearly what we're doing; two, not seeing clearly what we're doing brings about a negative or unpleasant outcome; and three, the unpleasant outcome produces tension which causes us not to see clearly what we're doing all over again.

In a circle or cycle there is no difference between the beginning and the end - they are the exact same point. Draw a circle on a sheet of paper and notice how the end returns to the beginning. The way it works physically is the way it works emotionally: Whenever you enter the moment tensely, you set events into motion which will bring about tension in the end. If you are in error going in you will be frustrated coming out; if correct going in you will be satisfied coming out. What goes, comes; what gives, gets. The end is always a mirror reflection of the beginning. The very state of mind or pocketbook you are in right now is the one you'll return to when all is said and done. Your future is nothing more than a projection of your present state of mind plus a few more gray hairs.

This is the basic principle, by the way, of how "fortune-tellers" can determine whether or not upcoming circumstances will be favorable for you. To the degree you are "read" to be calm and composed, your relationships or business activities would be expected to improve. But to the degree you appear nervous or emotional, the opposite is indicated - things will probably not go well. In which case, you would be advised not to make any important personal or business decisions at that particular time.

The remedy becomes this: change the beginning, change the present. Enter each moment calmly objective instead of tensely personal regardless of what happened a second ago or a year ago. It is simply a process of changing your attitude, changing the way you habitually look at things: it is not raining on you personally, it is just raining; that flat tire had nothing against the driver *as a person*, it just didn't like being driven over a spike; that clerk was not insensitive toward you personally, he or she just happened to be insensitive, and you just happened to be convenient. And that half glass of water isn't half empty or half full, it is just a half glass of water - period. The personal view is an *opinion*; the objective, universal view is a *fact*. Being relaxed and intelligent is not what you know; it's the matter-of-fact way you look at things.

It is this matter-of-fact, objective viewpoint that allows us to see the situation we are in with such extraordinary accuracy that fear, conflict, and error are naturally eliminated, and all of our actions and responses become perfectly appropriate, effective, and effortless.

Being objective is nothing more than common sense, and although not so common, it is our natural and original state of being; it is who and what we really are; it is the way we were before we let the pressures and influences of the world excite us off balance and out of control. Becoming objective is to regain that lost balance and self-control and along with it, our lost beauty, dignity, joy and power.

The purpose of the book, then, is to provide strategies and techniques for achieving and maintaining such a perspective.

PART ONE

THE PRINCIPLE OF BEING MENTALLY STILL

CHAPTER 1

BEING IMPARTIAL

Pride is the Original Imbalance and Source of Error

We were born self-centered, that is, with the inclination, bias or predisposition to take life in a personal way. But that is not our true nature; our true nature is to respond to life in an *im*personal way; it is to be balanced in outlook, not biased.

Self-centeredness is a disease we *acquired through inheritance* from our parents, who acquired it from theirs, and so on, all the way back to those who first developed the condition. Reversing or controlling this disease simply entails reversing or controlling our point of view.

How Self-Control Is Lost

Let's begin by seeing how taking life personally distorts our perception of reality, and in the process causes us to lose control of ourselves; that is to say, causes our reactions to be controlled externally.

Self-centeredness or self-consciousness, which is the same thing, comes accompanied by tension in the form of a paranoid-like pridefulness. *Paranoid* in the sense that we tend to feel that the disagreeable people we come across are against us *personally*, so we react with anger, resentment, or disturbance; and prideful in the sense that we're inclined to feel that the pleasing sort of person likes us personally, so we get a swelled head instead. Disagreeable people frazzle us, pleasant people flatter us; one drags us down, the other lifts us up.

In objective reality, however, people are inclined to act according to their *own* bias, disposition and peculiarities *regardless* of who they are with. The disagreeable person will tend to be so with *anyone* who happens across his path, and the pleasant person will tend to be so with whoever he is with as well.

Pride causes music to affect us similarly. We tend to take it personally or to identify with it so that depending on the arrangement and tempo, it can sentimentally sink us into melancholy or stir us to cheeriness and optimism. But music, like life itself, is a neutral, universal thing, so that whether its effect is negative or positive is entirely up to the individual listener and has nothing to do with the music itself or the creator himself.

It is because of this emotional swaying power of music that most commercial advertising on radio and television is produced in the form of musical jingles. The catchy tunes control our feelings and effectively hypnotize us into accepting or sympathizing with whatever product, person, or idea is being sold. We act according to how we feel. If our feelings can be controlled, then our actions can be controlled and what we buy or believe can be controlled.

Hypnosis is a simple two-step procedure of first, getting the subject's attention, and second, offering a suggestion. Through the medium of television, for example, our attention is gained through the excitement or stimulation of the senses (sensationalism). Through the sense of sight, our attention is captured by rapid-fire scenes of beautiful young people happily frolicking on the beach. And through the sense of hearing, our attention is held by the musical jingles and fast-talking salespeople.

Without such sophisticated entrancement or excitement techniques we would be more likely to see the product as it *really* is, rather than as we are being led to *imagine* or *believe* it is. We would see that the product's "image" and the actual product have very little in common, that there is nothing really romantic or exciting about a soft drink, for instance, that may consist of nothing more than gas, chemicals and tap water.

Such is the way taking life personally negatively affects our lives - by altering our perception of reality, and by controlling or influencing our reactions so that we are not really our own person, but an unconscious victim of circumstances "like a leaf being blown about in the wind."

To restate the vicious circle: Taking life personally is seeing things one-sidedly, distortedly. We're tense because we don't see the whole or true picture, and we don't because we are personally biased.

The balanced point of view, on the other hand, works in just the opposite way - it relates to clarity of perception and tranquillity of mind. Balance is seeing both sides of an experience with equal passion, like the pros and cons of a debate for instance. Clarity is seeing a thing in its wholeness and completeness, and tranquillity means not being disturbed or excited by one side any more than the other. You are composed because you see the *whole* situation, and you see the whole situation because you are *impartial.*

Impartialness is mentally centering yourself between the two opposite sides of any issue. It's taking a neutral position with respect to all that you experience whether it's external or internal, painful or pleasurable, negative or positive. To be balanced is like being in the position of a juror at a trial where fairness and justice depend on your ability to remain impartial. The prosecution is biased toward the state, the defense is biased toward the defendant; it is only for you, the juror, to remain indifferent. In order to make a fair judgment you must study the evidence presented by both sides with *equal* enthusiasm.

Life itself is like a trial in the sense that discovering truth is the whole object of it. It is to view the evidence of it, determine the facts of it, get to the heart of it. The prosecution and defense are like negative and positive thoughts and feelings, and we are the impartial observers, the neutral witnesses to these thoughts and feelings. The prosecuting thought says, "You are wrong," the defending thought says, "No, you are right." One says, "You are bad," the other, "You are good." One says, "Do this," the other, "No, do that." Who shall you believe? You cannot believe either because both are biased opinions so are irrelevant, immaterial and incompetent. Through maintaining a balanced perspective, we rise above internal conflict and allow the truth of a thing to become revealed, and the way to go to become obvious.

Whenever you have conflicted feelings about something, it's because you are looking at it one-sidedly; you are somehow being partial or prejudiced in your viewpoint. If you are having mixed feelings over whether or not to have a hot fudge sundae, it is because your heart is partial and your mind is prejudiced, or vice versa. There is a division, a split, a conflict which indicates the wrong time to act - not because the mind is superior in judgment to the heart, or that the heart is superior to the mind - but because there is an imbalance operating. And whenever there is imbalance, there will be error. Here your heart says "Yes, a sundae would be just wonderful," but your mind says "No, no, don't do it. Think of the calories; think of how many miles you will have to run to pay for it; think of what a new wardrobe of large-sized clothing would cost!" But deep down the choice has already been made. Sure, you will rationalize it, intellectualize it, consider it from every possible angle - but we both know that the hot fudge sundae is going to come out on top. It's like placing the sundae before a kangaroo court where it's given a "fair" trial before being eaten.

Stillness Causes Clarity

Clarity comes from seeing a situation in its *wholeness*, seeing a situation in its wholeness comes from staying *centered* in the middle of it, and staying centered requires that the mind be *still*.

Seeing a thing wholly and completely is like the superior view the manager of a company has over his subordinates in the various departments. The manager of a hotel, for instance, is aware of all the different aspects of a hotel's operation and how they are related to each other. The hotel is an organization with the manager centered or balanced between all its functions. The front desk, housekeeping, sales, maintenance, accounting, and food and beverage departments are all on the periphery. Each department is biased, so to speak; that is, each sees only its own narrow, limited *part* of the operation and is blind to the other parts, while the manager has a *view of the whole*.

Being centered between extremes is like the lifeguard who, standing *still at the center* of the beach, the point of maximum visibility, is more effective than the one who moves back and forth from one extreme end to the other. The "centered" lifeguard sees the *whole* beach at *all* times; the "extreme" (biased) lifeguard sees only *part* of the beach at a time while always leaving the opposite part unattended.

The mind that is still sees clearly, while the mind that moves sees distortedly. The mind works like a pair of binoculars or a camera in the sense that the more still it is held, the clearer the view or sharper the image.

In another sense, the mind works like a chimney and damper. When the damper (the viewpoint) is straight up and down (impartial), the smoke (what you see and hear) can flow without being altered. But to the degree the damper is leaning to the left or to the right (being partial or prejudiced), it blocks the free passage of smoke. And while it's blocking it, it's also distorting it. Instead of the smoke passing directly and immediately out, it must now twist or contort itself around the damper so that the smoke that now comes out of the chimney is a somewhat different shape than the smoke that went in.

The Mind Is Merely A Medium

All that we perceive must pass through the mind in order to be understood. The mind, like the chimney and damper, functions as a tunnel or conduit through which information may pass from one point to another. The mind, of itself, is not supposed to *do* anything, it is only a *medium*. Its job is to remain as balanced as possible, as "straight up and down" as possible. That is its most unobtrusive position. It is then, in effect, not there at all, as when air currents turn a hanging mobile or placard sideways so that it seems to have disappeared. As far as the smoke is then concerned, there is no damper. The smoke can now pass without interference and without its nature or character being altered in the process.

We want high-fidelity perception. We don't want what we see and hear to be affected on the way to our understanding. We want to get exactly what we see, and see exactly what we're getting. When the letter carrier delivers our mail he doesn't open it to correct the grammar or rewrite it to make it sound better - he delivers it *as is*.

To Be Centered Is To Be Unaffected

To be impartial is to be composed, self-controlled, unaffected. To illustrate, think of yourself as being a children's see-saw, just a straight board. When you are a balanced see-saw, you are unaffected by extremes of "ups" and "downs" because when a part of you goes up, the opposite part of you goes down to an equal degree so that your "straightness" or "integrity" is never violated; that is to say, you never get "all bent out of shape." The weight or influence on one end, cancels out the influence on the opposite end, for a net affect on you of *zero*.

And what is true physically, is true morally and emotionally: When you are centered, the "good" part of you cancels out the "bad" part of you; what is "right" about you balances out what is "wrong" about you; what is "pleasurable" cancels what is "painful," and so on with all pairs of opposites or complements. As far as you, the impartial see-saw, are concerned, there is no good or bad, right or wrong, pain or pleasure. Such things are relative and exist only to the degree you choose to sit on that particular extreme.

Being unaffected is like being in the position of a real estate broker or middleman whose living comes from the transaction itself, so is indifferent to the personalities of the buyers and sellers involved. It makes no difference if Mr. Pain is the buyer and Mr. Pleasure is the seller, or vice versa - Mr. Middleman still gets paid. But on the other hand, if Mr. Middleman only knows Mr. Pleasure and not Mr. Pain, or vice versa, then the situation would be imbalanced, no sale could take place, and Mr. Middleman *would* be affected.

Similarly, the owner of a race track is unaffected by the amounts won or lost by virtue of his middleman position. Every dollar won is balanced by a dollar lost. After expenses, the proceeds from the losers are equally divided among the winners. The negative effect of the winning tickets is cancelled out by the positive effect of the losing tickets. The owner remains calm and content. He is indifferent to whether you win or lose; it's all the same to him. His only concern is that you play the game. For the middleman, the centered man, there is no winning or losing; there is only the joy and profit of the transaction.

Freedom from affectation, then, involves cultivating an equal appreciation for both winning and losing, for both pain and pleasure, knowing that both are necessary to the transaction of life. Life is such that sometimes you will win and sometimes lose; sometimes there will be pleasure and sometimes pain; sometimes you'll be the buyer and sometimes the seller. They are two equal and inseparable sides of the same coin so that being affected by one side more than the other is incompatible with reality. As life includes both, our embrace must include both, for it is we who *are* life.

No, you cannot even have a *preference* for winning, a *preference* for pleasure, a *preference* for sunshine. Preferences are the very cause of the anxiety and stress that block joy and achievement. Simply point your nose in the direction of your goal and go about your business creatively instead of emotionally. Know what your role, task or purpose is at any given moment and involve yourself in it to the fullest of your ability. If it turns out negative, don't be disturbed by it for disturbance will prevent you from seeing the mistake you made. If it turns out positive, don't get excited for the tension of success will prevent you from maintaining it or repeating it.

Holding a preference (being partial) has the same negative effect as being pressured. When you hold a preference for something, you are unnecessarily putting pressure on yourself, which is just as bad as being externally pressured. To be pressured is to be tilted off balance which causes you to get the opposite of what you wanted. Pressure at school, for example, will disturb your concentration; pressure from a member of your family will poison your relationship; pressure at work will stifle your creativity; pressure to produce or perform will cause impotence; pressure to conform will cause you to rebel; pressure to stop a bad habit will strengthen its grip on you; financial pressure will block your ability to create money, and so on. (This principle is sometimes called the law of reverse effort, and we'll discuss it more fully in Chapter Four.) A balanced perspective means you don't have a preference, a partiality, a prejudice, or a pressure, so you function more fully, efficiently, naturally, and effortlessly.

Those who claim to operate better under pressure are really unconsciously addicted to it. The person who *needs* pressure in order to function is one who is wrongly motivated. The rightly motivated person works first for the *work itself*, that is, for the *action itself*. Prosperity then follows as a natural side effect. But the wrongly motivated person has it backwards: he works for the side effect - the money first! He has a problem, for once he is financially comfortable, there is no longer any real reason to be productive, so he must create artificial pressure through cultivating a taste for more and more expensive toys, entertainments, and forms of business speculation or gambling. Thus he spins in a circle like a mouse on a spending- to-earn-earning-to-spend treadmill. Once he arrives at each new plateau, he crashes into the reality of the unfulfillment and emptiness of it. He finds higher and higher mountains to climb only to end up where he began - nowhere. Only if he lives long enough does he come to realize that the top is not where "it" is at; where it's at is in the *journey*; it's in the *action*; it is *enroute*. It is always in the exact spot where he happens to be standing at any given moment. The top of the mountain is not a place; it is a state of mind right here and now.

There are not different kinds of tension, only one, but that one is felt in various ways. There is the painful tension of worry, guilt, fear, and anger; and the pleasurable tension of sexuality, a moving drama, a majestic symphony, the birth of a child, adventure, discovery, etc. Tension itself is neutral energy, but becomes negative when we get carried away, and becomes positive when kept under control, that is, kept neutral. When under control we still feel the whole spectrum of human emotion and we feel it even more vividly, but we are not excited or disturbed by it.

Balance controls physical, mental, and spiritual energy so we can operate and grow more efficiently. Physical balance, such as pacing ourselves during physical activity, controls energy so we can act and do things more efficiently; mental balance, such as stilling the mind, conserves psychic energy so we can think more efficiently. (The nature of the body is to move, but the nature of the mind is to be still. If the body isn't exercised, its muscles will atrophy; if the mind isn't stilled, intelligence will atrophy.) And spiritual balance is controlling our emotions so we can feel or perceive reality more efficiently - reality or truth being here defined as that which exists *before* we pesonalize it, intellectualize it, or emotionalize it.

Now the only difference between being emotional and being spiritual is that in the one case, you're *out* of control, and in the other, *in* control. The emotional person is scattered, the spiritual person is collected; the emotional person is possessed by the world, the spiritual person is self- possessed; the emotional person is excited by everything but can find nothing to interest him, the spiritual person is interested in everything but excited by nothing; the emotional person is a slave - for whatever excites us, owns us, the spiritual person is free; the emotional person is disconnected from his soul, so is easily suggestible; the spiritual person is connected to the center of his being so is firm and confident as to who he is and what he is about.

Balance: The Original State Of Easiness

The word *excite* comes from the Latin *exciere* which means *to move away*. The Latin *relaxare*, on the other hand, means *to loosen back*. To *loosen* means *to make less severe or tense*; *to relieve from effort*; *to make easy*. And *back* means *to be restored to a previous condition*. When we're *re*laxing, then, we are *re*turning to our original state of easiness-which is the state of balance. Balance is our home, our ideal, our center of operations. Whenever we leave it, we feel discomfort, and whenever we return, we feel at ease. Excitement is what moves us away from that center, and relaxation is what brings us back.

Being affected with disturbance or excitement indicates three things: one, that we have put all our emotional eggs in one basket, which is just as imprudent spiritually as it is materially; two, that we have yet to see or accept the ever-changing, up and down, indefinite nature of reality. Emotional affectedness is really a subtle expression of insecurity over not being able to control things. But insecurity is a concealed blessing, for if we were able to control the actions and responses of people and things, life would be unbearably boring. Who would enjoy making love or conversation with a person whose every response was predetermined? What fun or profit could there be in playing a game in which everyone knew in advance what the outcome would be? And how could the stock and commercial markets function if everyone knew their movements in advance? Security is not the way the world works either materially or spiritually. It is insecurity, and only insecurity that makes all the games and transactions of life both interesting and workable.

Insecurity is the only thing in the world that doesn't change, so is the only thing we *can* depend on, and the only thing that will bring relaxation and happiness. If security is what you want, then, paradoxically, it is only through *in*security that you will be able to find it. And the way to live in insecurity is to live in total and unconditional acceptance of all that exists whether good, bad, right, wrong, painful, or pleasurable.

And the third thing, is that in order to *become* affected, you have to *already be* affected. In order to become disturbed or excited in the second place, you must already be disturbed or excited in the first place. You can't become something unless it is already latent within you. The emotionally affected person is like a nervous mouse trap just waiting around for a rude mouse to come along and set him off.

BEING IMPARTIAL

Balance comes by degree, and to the degree you are balanced in outlook, you transcend being emotionally affected by things. On a lower level, you would be unaffected by rain or sunshine; on a higher level, you would remain unaffected even if that rain brought you financial disaster. Your essential good nature would not change and you would not jump from the roof of a building. Your wife, children, and dog might leave you, your friends might look at you sideways, the bank may take your home,and the Internal Revenue Service may padlock your business. You might even have to sleep in a public shelter and stand in soup lines, but none of these things would distress you. You would remain your calm and composed self. External conditions could not corrupt the real you, the beautiful you, the eternally elegant and courageous you.

Of course, being so calm and clear you wouldn't come to such extreme circumstances. You would have foreseen or anticipated the problems, or if not, you would have had the creative power to make the necessary course corrections and bounce back. But the point is to become less and less affected by more and more things until you come to realize that nothing external can harm you, that it's only when you allow outside influences to get under your skin that all your problems begin, that even if you were at rock bottom you would still be all right, you would still survive, that you had always survived and that you always would, that there is indeed nothing to fear, that all that *appears* negative in life doesn't exist in reality but is merely an illusion born of an imbalanced outlook.

With higher degrees of unaffectedness pain becomes less and less painful until you cannot tell the difference between it and pleasure. The dividing line between them diminishes until it disappears, and you are not sure whether you are supposed to laugh or cry. There are no more ups and downs - they become equal. The mountains lower and the valleys lift. Now there is only one, not two. You have risen above all superficial distinctions of pain and pleasure, failure and success. Now there remains only enjoyment and serenity.

Balance Is Flexibility

To live in a non-personal way is to have a ball by being a ball. A ball can't be emotionally affected because, being round, it has no sides or positions it can be partial to or prejudiced against. A ball is equal on all sides, the same all around. It can roll with equal ease in any direction the situation happens to be slanting. A ball cannot land wrong side up or upside down because it has no such divisions. When you are a ball, there's only one way you can ever land - and that's right side up. To be impartial, then, is to be a ball; to be biased, is to be a square.

Being round enables you to roll with the punches of the world. Whenver you stand flat-footed or in a fixed position, the slightest tap rattles your brains. In order to be unaffected by the world, your head and the world's fist must move, not toward each other, and not away from each other either, but in the same direction at the same time - more as if you were dancing rather than fighting.

Given the hardness of the world and the softness of your head, wisdom demands a response to life that is a little more sympathetic to the world. To roll with the punches is not to compete with the world, but to cooperate with it, to harmonize with it, to be in tune with it, in relationship with it. When the orchestra is playing a tango, then dance the tango, not the Watusi; when at a funeral, be somber not cheerful; when at a wedding, be cheerful not somber. You do not tell the world what to do; the world, that is, the situation, tells you what to do.

My friend Maxie Pierpont lost his job as a waiter-trainee as a result of not understanding this principle of rolling or floating with the situation as opposed to being stuck in one position:

He was balancing a large tray of fruit cocktails on one hand while serving them to guests with the other, when for the third time that evening the tray and dishes tipped over and crashed to the floor.

When the manager came to investigate, Maxie explained that he was holding the tray at the exact center just as he was told, but that after he had served one or two, the tray just tipped over by itself.

"But didn't you keep shifting your hand to compensate for the changing distribution of weight?" asked the manager. "Didn't you keep re-centering your position?"

"No," said Maxie, "I was only trained to hold the tray at its center."

"But the point of balance isn't a *fixed* point"; said the manager, "it isn't a *particular* place. If the tray were empty, yes, the point of balance *would* be at its center, but the tray is not alone in the world; it lives in relationship with the dishes. So the center must be flexible to accommodate their spontaneous comings and goings. Every time a dish is removed from the tray it is a different situation, so you must move your hand to the new point of balance."

"I didn't know you had to be an engineer to wait on tables," replied Maxie. Whereupon he was politely asked to turn in his apron and leave the premises.

Pride operates under the misconception that *he* is the center of all experience, that everything revolves around *him*. In reality, the *situation* is the center, not us personally. We are merely the actors, the players, the participants. The situation is the thing. Or in Shakespeare's words, "The play is the thing." We are nothing, the situation is everything. The transaction is where the action is. Pride is *self*-centered while balance is *situation*-centered; balance has no self while pride is full of himself; pride is stuck on himself while balance is free of himself.

Being Calmly Excited

Now we don't want to, nor can we, eliminate our emotions because emotion is inherent in the flesh. What we do want to do is control them. Either we control them or they control us, and the way we control them is to be relaxed *while* excited. Our usual pattern is to constantly bounce back and forth between excitement and relaxation like a ping-pong ball. Something moves us and *later* we calm down from it - tension then calmness then tension then calmness. Our goal is to move the excitement part of the cycle and the relaxation part closer and closer together until they overlap or occur simultaneously. We want to be composed *as* we move like a ballet dancer who can flit freely about the stage while maintaining a graceful and dignified balance at every step of the way. Being composed and excited at the same time is a process similar to that of walking up a down escalator where excitement is at the bottom and relaxation is at the top. In order to stay centered between them, we must walk up at the exact same speed as the escalator is moving down. In this way we remain still *while* moving, calm *while* excited; in this way we can fully experience both the painful and the pleasurable without being negatively effected by either.

The Positive Principle Of Being Impartial

The question becomes, what is our mood when we see all things with equal eyes? What is our mood, for instance, when unaffected by both pain and pleasure? The mood is one of *pleasure*. Whenever we are centered between opposing emotions we automatically take on the mood of the *positive* one. When balanced between doubt and confidence, we become confident; between resentment and tolerance, we become tolerant or forgiving; between guilt and innocence, we feel innocent, and likewise with all that we feel.

The positive pole always dominates in a balanced situation because it is the pole most compatible with our true nature. Human nature is essentially positive because life itself is positive - positive in the sense that it is whole, complete, real, perfectly organized and perfectly ordered. So to the degree you are balanced in outlook, you become whole, complete, real, organized and orderly yourself. You become compatible with life instead of at odds with it; consequently, the positive is what you will naturally feel and express. This principle can be likened to the traffic law which says that when two vehicles approach an intersection at the same time (in balance), the one on the right (the positive one) has the right of way (becomes dominant).

But when your perspective is imbalanced, you block out a part of yourself like a cloud blocks the sun. And in so doing, become, in effect, incomplete, unwhole, unreal, disorganized and disordered. I say "in effect" because the sun is not *really* gone, just *blocked*. This incompleteness and unwholeness, etc., is experienced as an emptiness, a hollowness, a boredom, an unfulfillment, or a deficiency which we term "negative." The crucial thing to grasp here is that such negativity is false; it has no basis in reality. It is merely an appearance, an emotional optical illusion that is corrected when we shift from a personal angle of vision to a more universal one.

A Double-Barreled Balancing Technique

Becoming impartial or indifferent is a simple three-step procedure: first, it is knowing what your present mood is; second, it is knowing what the opposite mood is; and third, it is moving between them by either *denying them both or accepting them both*. Let us say you are feeling angry or resentful toward someone or something. First *know* that that's how you're feeling. Then, consider what the opposite of resentment is. The opposite is to forgive, to overlook, or to be tolerant. The third step, denying both or accepting both, is accomplished as follows: In denying both, don't overlook the offense and at the same time don't resent it either; in accepting both, you resent and overlook simultaneously. In other words, be neither or be both, but don't be partial or prejudiced; don't be divided or conflicted.

Here is the principle behind how this technique works: According to elementary physics there can be no such thing as a total vacuum; so when you are neither resentful nor tolerant - something will have to give. Either the positive aspect will be pressed forward or the negative, and as we have seen, it is the positive that will emerge as the dominant expression.

The other barrel of the technique works according to a complementary law which says that two things cannot occupy the same space at the same time. When you are both resentful and tolerant at the same time, again, something will have to give. The same positive principle of balance comes into play whereby the positive "tolerance" cancels out the negative "resentment" for a net result of *zero*-just like a balance scale. And the zero state, like the vacuum state above, will express the positive, making the spirit of tolerance or forgiveness the governing mood.

Knowing The Cause Frees You From The Effect

Continuing with the resentment/tolerance example, let's see how these theoretical considerations apply in practice.

Overlooking the offensiveness of others is, again, based on the reality that how a person behaves is *his* problem not yours. If a patient in an insane asylum insulted you, would you become upset? Of course not because you would know the cause of his behavior is his imbalance and not you personally. Knowledge of his insanity would balance out the effect of the insult so you'd come away undisturbed. Now suppose you were at a social gathering and were offered a similar insult - perhaps someone commented on how nicely your outfit clashed. Would you then react with anger? It would be inappropriate for the same reason as above - that the cause of the rudeness is mental imbalance and has nothing to do with you personally. The imbalance here will, of course, be less obvious than in the above instance but the difference is merely one of setting and degree - imbalance remains the case.

You would not react with anger but you might respond by excusing yourself to "check in with the babysitter," or you might inquire as to what the person's favorite color combinations *are*, or you might respond by punching the person on the nose - depending on the circumstances. The point is, that you don't do it with anger; you don't do it as an emotional reaction to the *person*, but as a composed response to the *situation*. The difference is that in the one case, you are out of control, and in the other, in control. The rule of thumb is this: whatever you do emotionally will be incorrect; whatever you do impersonally will be correct.

Reacting with anger effectively makes you imbalanced too by pulling you away from your own center of poise. Through emotional reaction in general, and anger in particular, the dis-ease of another is transferred to you. You complete the transaction the other initiates. The insensitive person, consciously or unconsciously, is offering you of his offensiveness - will you accept? That is the question. He is attempting to sell you something - will you buy? It takes two to complete a sale. If you react emotionally, then you become his customer, his market, his dupe. You put yourself in the same league with him. You are playing his game, on his level, and by his rules. He is now controlling you, exploiting you, dominating you. You are not longer in possession of yourself, no longer your own person but have become subject to him. He acts and you re-act; he is the cause and you are the effected; he is the mover and you are the moved.

The self-centered person, consciously or unconsciously, gets his gratification through causing you to react to him in some way. He needs you. Your being affected by him gives him his kick; it is his egotistical livelihood. He depends on your emotional reaction to feel good about his inferior self. He needs to get a rise out of you. He glows with prideful satisfaction whenever he is able to move you into reacting to him. Your emotional reaction gives him his vitality while it is simultaneously drained from you. He is a user. He lifts himself up by dragging you down. But without your reaction, he is nothing; without your reaction, he shrivels into impotence - for nothing can have power over you unless you give it, and you give it by reacting emotionally.

Whenever we are affected by anyone the tendency is to turn around and likewise affect others. It is to grossly or subtlely, knowingly or unknowingly, impose our values, beliefs, problems, or diseases on others. It is being miserable and wanting to spread it around; it is hurting another because someone hurt you, stealing from another because someone stole from you. It is being envious of those above you and scornful of those below you; it is being impatient with your children because your husband was impatient with you because his boss was impatient with him, and so on. It is taking our frustrations out on those around us who are most vulnerable, and being victimized by those to whom we are most vulnerable. Thus, being emotionally affected, and then reacting by affecting others, is what degenerates us into an uncivilized, dog-eat-dog society.

The Principles Of Love And Wisdom

Being impartial means not allowing any person, place, or thing to affect or interfere with your being yourself - this is called *wisdom*; and conversely, it means not affecting or interfering with the being of another - this is called *love*. Love is how we act toward others, wisdom is how we respond to others. This is just the opposite of the above situation. When we remain emotionally unaffected, we are sensitive not to emotionally affect others. Love and wisdom are a team, two sides of the same coin. It is the ancient adage to "live and let live" or "be and let be." Love lets you be *your*self; wisdom lets me be *my*self.

To not interfere with the free expression of another is to be sensitive, discreet, and unobtrusive. A child at play is natural and spontaneous, that is, until an overbearing parent or teacher comes too close, then he becomes stifled, self-conscious. He then begins to wonder if he's doing something wrong, bad, or if he's violating some rule or other and won't be approved of. His mind has entered the picture so that he is no longer *really* playing but is now *acting* like he is playing. The spontaneity is gone; the actions are now false and premeditated. What was natural is now studied and affected. The same applies in all relationships - that to the degree we are obtrusive or domineering we inhibit a person's freedom of expression.

Not interfering with the being of another involves spontaneously accepting that person as the sovereign individual he is without any conditions or reservations whatsoever. The relaxed person is without judgment or expectation. Being whole and complete, he has no ulterior motives, nothing to lose, and nothing to prove. He has nothing to do but be still and act as an invisible mirror or screen upon which another may freely project his soul without fear of unsolicited advice, comment or criticism.

Since the relaxed person no longer has a self, that is to say, since he no longer has a self-ish or personal viewpoint, his enjoyment comes through your enjoyment. To the degree you are delighted, he is delighted, and you will be delighted to the degree you can express yourself freely.

Love, then, has nothing to do with emotion - *love is the very absence of emotion*. This doesn't mean that love is without passion - it is infinitely passionate, but the passion is for life, for the situation, for the *other* person. Emotion is selfish, needy, dependent, possessive. Love is beyond need; it is free and independent; it doesn't seek to own you, use you, control you, or change you - it only seeks to be sensitive and responsive to you.

Not allowing yourself to become tense is being good to yourself, it's loving yourself; not causing tension for others is being good to them, it's loving them. This is the master key to health, happiness, and personal effectiveness. When the great teachers of humanity spoke of love, it wasn't because love was "nice," it was because love *works*; it was because love is powerful and practical, the most powerful and practical thing in existence. And to be impartial in your perspective is to be this love, this wisdom, this power.

CHAPTER 2

UNIVERSAL LAW

*The **P**rinciple of **O**neness is an **I**mmutable **S**ystem of **E**quilibrium*

Balance is indicated for the individual because balance is how the universe works as a whole. Whatever works for the whole works for the part, and whatever works for the part works for the whole. We are not separate from the universe in any way but are a microcosm, a miniature of it in every way. The universe is a whole pie and we are a little slice. All the ingredients of the whole are included in the part, so how it tastes is how we taste; how it works is how we work. There is no difference in substance, only in size.

The universe works successfully in that it supports and sustains life. We are alive, therefore it works. If we dissect it to isolate the principal factor behind its success, we find that it is balance. *The universe is the government and balance is its constitutional law.*

That something is universal means it applies in every direction and on all levels. A universal joint is one that can turn in any direction; a universal wrench is one that can be operated from any position. That the law of balance is universal means that it applies in every department of life. We can find balance at work reducing tension and increasing efficiency everywhere, not only on the material, psychological and emotional levels but also morally, economically, politically, socially, ecologically, and so on.

To name just a few: the balance of power between national alliances relaxes political tension; the balance between church and state relaxes ideological tension; the balanced budget within a country, and the balance of trade between countries reduces economic tension; the balance between plants and animals and their food and water reduces ecological tension; the stock and commercial markets are "relaxed" when there is a balance between buyers and sellers or supplies and demands. We seek to balance our losses with profits, our liabilities with assets, our expenses with income; justice in the court is based on balance between prosecution and defense; our decision to buy a thing is not based on price alone or quality alone, but on the balance between them. In labor relations we strive to balance the needs of both employees and employers; in politics, balance is maintained by the pushing and pulling activities of the Democrats and Republicans, the "left" and the "right," the liberals and conservatives; the success of a constitutional government is based on maintaining balance between the executive, legislative, and judicial branches; and so on, indefinitely. Thus the world is an orderly, harmonious structure with balance the central organizing principle, the direction toward which all things move.

The Universal Success Formula

This law of balance not only orders the *direction* of all activity, but orders the *form* and *function* of everything that exists as well. It determines a thing's structure and its use. For example, the front half of a sheet of paper is balanced by its back half, and it's because of this balanced form that it can now be used to write on. The inside half of a tea cup is balanced by its outside half, and it is by virtue of this balanced form that the cup can now function as a container.

This balanced nature of all things is such an obvious fact of existence that we commonly fail to notice it. All things must have two opposite aspects: Every "inner" is balanced by an "outer"; every "front" must have a "back"; every "up," a "down"; every "this," a "that"; there cannot be a "good" without a "bad," a "right" without a "wrong," a "pleasure" without a "pain." Balance is what makes a thing whole and complete and can be expressed in a simple mathematical equation: one-half plus one-half equals a whole (.5 + .5 = 1). Let's look at this equation for a minute and then see how it applies to human nature.

Notice that this formula, which we'll refer to as the "universal success formula," has *three* aspects to it not two, and that it takes *three* aspects to make a thing whole and complete: one thing plus another thing *equals a third thing.* The third thing is the sum, result, or offspring of the first two. The inside half of a cup plus the outside half, make a *whole* cup. The "head" half of a coin plus the "tail" half, equal a *whole* coin; the negative half of a battery plus the positive half, form a *complete* circuit. If a thing doesn't have these *three* aspects, it either doesn't exist or it doesn't work.

How does this "universal success formula" apply to us personally? What are the three aspects that constitute man? In other words, who are we? The first thing we are is *Life* - we are alive; the second thing we are is *Consciousness*, we are conscious of being alive, and the third thing is the result of the first two - the third thing is *Bliss.* Awareness of the existence of life *results* in happiness. Life *plus* consciousness *equals* bliss. They are the three interrelated institutions that form our true self, our true nature. They are all we are; they are who, what, and how we are; they are the essential elements that identify us as being human.

"Life" is the first part of the formula. It has to do with creative power, force, energy, vitality. It is the body, the physical part of us, the part that moves and acts. It is the "male" principle of movement and outgoingness.

"Consciousness" was second in order of appearance; it is the second part of the formula. First, there was life, then we became aware of it. Consciousness has to do with the mind; it is the mental, psychological, thinking aspect of us. It is knowledge, wisdom, understanding, intelligence. It is the "female" principle of stillness and receptiveness.

"Bliss," the third part of our nature, is the fulfillment of the equation. Bliss is the purpose and function of life just as being a container is the function of a tea cup. Bliss is the fruit of the union, the product of the marriage between "life" and consciousness." Consciousness "knew" life and conceived a child whose name was bliss. Bliss is of the heart, soul, or center; it is the spiritual aspect; it is love, happiness, joyousness and delight. It is the part of us that speaks, feels and desires.

This bliss or love aspect of our nature is most readily observed in the relationship between parent and offspring, especially among animals. Look at the loving tenderness of a cat toward her kittens, so natural and instinctive. Every cell in her body is a love cell. The kittens are bathed in it. Almost immediately after birth, they are at care-free play. Sensing the existence of love and feeling its presence about them, they respond with boundless joy. Their attitude seems to be that if love exists, what could there be to fear.

Wholeness is being all three of these qualities simultaneously. It's being alive, aware of it, and happy about it all at the same time. We cannot be conscious of life and remain unhappy, and we cannot be happy while unconscious of life. *If a person is unhappy, unsatisfied, unfulfilled, it's simply because he's unconscious.*

The Creation Of Consciousness

The purpose of balance is to awaken consciousness. That was its purpose in the beginning and that is its purpose now. To illustrate, let's turn the evolutionary clock back to our embryonic stage - when we were alive, but not yet conscious of it (which is very similar to the state we're in right now).

In the beginning, life existed, and *we* were it. We were alive but weren't aware of it yet. We were as if in a state of sleep where all of our vital functions continued to operate and develop without conscious involvement. The time *would* come when we would awaken to the fact of life's existence, but first, certain conditions would have to mature or evolve. We were like a seed which inherently contained the complete blueprint of what it could become, but in order to germinate and bloom to that potential, we must first be exposed to the right mixture of nourishing soil, sun and water.

Our goal and creative task, then, as a budding young organism would be to somehow evolve those conditions which would allow our consciousness to awaken.

The main problem, or rather, the *catch* to be overcome in accomplishing this goal will have to do with a certain law of relativity or relationship. This law says that knowledge is a relative thing meaning that *we cannot know anything unless in relation or contrast with its opposite.* The "opposite" provides the contrast necessary to make a think stand out and be noticed. Opposites act like mirrors that reveal each others' presence. For example, we wouldn't notice pleasure without pain. If it weren't for intermittant pain we wouldn't recognize pleasure. Pain is the very thing that makes pleasure so pleasing. Pain, then, not only opposes pleasure, but complements it as well. They are two sides of the same coin. Wherever there is sameness we fail to notice; we cannot discriminate: A polar bear lying in the snow is very difficult to see; we don't notice the hair style of a person we see everyday until it's been changed; we don't notice the homes on our own street because the sameness of the scene has dulled our awareness. It is only when a house has been re-painted or removed that we realize it had ever existed. It is contrast that stimulates awareness. Similarly, we wouldn't know day as being "day" unless it alternated with "night"; we wouldn't know cold as being "cold" unless there was such a thing as "warm" to compare it with; we wouldn't know a mountain as being a mountain unless there was a corresponding valley, and so on with all pairs of opposites - including life and death. And therein was our problem - that in order to *know* life, we would have to *know* death!

What to do? It seems illogical, contradictory. When death is reached, it would be too late to experience life because then we would be dead - that is, unless we somehow came to life at the point of death - which is exactly what happens: There is a split moment during the life to death transition when this law of relationship is fulfilled and an awakening of consciousness occurs. It is that split second when life is leaving but has not yet left, and when death is approaching but has not yet arrived. In between them is a tiny crossover point, a point of transcendence, a paradoxical moment when there is *neither* life nor death, and at the exact same time there is *both* life and death. They overlap or superimpose each other so that, in effect, each contains the quality of the other at the same time. It's like a composite or "trick" photograph that's produced by overlapping different negatives. Or it's like a person straddling the border line between two states, whereby, he is at the same time in *both* states and in *neither* state; he is balanced or poised between them.

It is of course a moment of infinitesimal subtlety and duration like the moment when a ball thrown into the air is no longer rising, but has not yet begun to fall. It is simultaneously not rising and not falling and at the same time it is rising and is falling. It is balanced in the middle, poised between the "up" and the "down." The ball has attained to a state of equilibrium. The centrifugal force which threw the ball up is now equal to the gravitational force which would bring it down. The ball has now, in effect, transcended time and space: it is neither in the past nor the future; it is neither moving nor still; it is neither up nor down. It is in this vacuum, this void, this state of *balanced stillness* that an awakening of consciousness occurs.

The problem to overcome, then, was that *real* death was not very practical to use as an opposite or mirror through which to see that we were alive.

The solution became this: *create the illusion or effect of death*. This could be accomplished by creating a universe with a system of equilibrium that exactly duplicates that state of "balanced stillness" - *but on an ongoing, continuous basis instead of for just a split-second.*

Constructing A Balanced Universe

In the beginning, we didn't have a "physical" body, at least, not one as coarse as we have now. At that time, we consisted of a fine ethereal substance of incredible malleability. Gold, for instance, is so ductile that an ounce of it can be drawn into a thin strand of wire over a mile long. But the essential substance of our being is so exquisitely fine, that a dot less than the size of the period at the end of this sentence was drawn into a single unbroken strand that filled up all the space in the entire universe.

When we were only a dot just beginning to come out of ourself to begin construction of a relative universe, we quickly realized that we could conserve energy by moving in the form of an up and down wave-like pattern instead of in a straight line: We stretched in one direction then rested an equivalent period in the opposite direction. We stretched and rested, stretched and rested. The opposites of "movement" and "rest" perfectly complemented each other. But the more marvelous thing about this strategy was that we stretched even during the rest part of the cycle and rested during the stretching part. It wasn't that we moved and *then* rested, we moved and rested simultaneously. We rested *while* moving and moved *while* resting. The gravity of the "down" movement built up so much momentum, like a speeding roller coaster, that instead of stopping at the bottom, it just continued up to the peak of the next cycle where gravity pulled it down again to repeat the process all over again.

The centrifugal force of the "up" movement perfectly balanced the gravitational force of the "down" rest. We vibrated forward in the same way that a fish wiggles forward. It is this wonderfully efficient system of simultaneous movement and rest that allowed us to fill up the entire universe without effort or drain of energy.

For an indeterminate period of time afterward we just moved about in a seemingly chaotic manner, in, around, and through ourself like dough in a gigantic, slow-motion mixing machine until all of a sudden we formed ourself into a state of perfect equilibrium in which we became like the "zero" point at the center of a balance scale where all the influences on our left became equal to all those on our right "balancing out" the effects of each other in the process.

We took up the whole universe yet it was like we weren't there at all. Our weight balanced itself right out. We were so equally balanced, so equally opposed, so equally distributed, that we became, in effect, invisible. Every "this" cancelled every "that"; a "surplus" here balanced a "shortage" there; an "action" here caused a "reaction" there; every "cause" produced an "effect" and every effect had a cause; every giving, received and every taking, diminished. It was one unified, balanced, interconnected, interrelated, harmonious whole. And at the center of it all, at the heart of it all, poised in between all opposing influences, in a state of perfect stillness and freedom, was where we were.

At that moment, we awoke. Consciousness dawned on us. For a while we just stood there, as when we sometimes awaken from a sleep and don't quite realize it immediately but just stare out blankly for some time before knowing, "Oh, I'm awake." We looked out with our eyes of understanding now open and realized that we were alive, that we were living, that life was happening and it was happening through us. We were the medium of life and simultaneously, a witness to it as well. And since we were all there was, our perception was all pervasive and all knowing. We were as if made of the purest crystal, seeming not to be there at all, yet present everywhere. We were at once on the outside looking in and on the inside looking out; at once the subject and the object; at once the beginning and the end.

For a sense of this experience, imagine yourself standing at the center of a vast, empty desert of sand. All around you for as far as the eye can see, there is only level ground meeting a wide open, cloudless sky at a huge circular horizon. It is like being in the top half of a great blue bubble. Now, while remaining calm, allow the entire ground you're standing on to completely disappear so that the bottom half of the bubble meets the top half with you just floating in the middle of a peaceful sea of blueness. The sky is no longer just up but is now everywhere; it is all around you. You are now *in* the sky. Now, while remaining very alert, allow your entire body to disappear so that all that remains is consciousness. The final umbilical cord has been severed. There are no more boundaries, no more separations or distinctions. You are no longer *in* the sky, now you *are* the sky. There is no difference between you and the sky. You have become one with it, one with all that exists.

To the knowledge that we were alive, we could only respond with a bliss whose glow lovingly pervaded the whole universe. "Oh, the sweetness of it, the utter gloriousness of it. I am a living thing. Something is, and I am that which is; I am that. A great mirror has folded in two revealing that I AM."

CHAPTER 3

THE POWER OF RELAXATION

*The **P**urpose of **O**beying **I**nner **S**tillness is **E**ffectiveness*

The three qualities of aliveness, intelligence, and happiness that we consist of lie latent just below the surface of the subconscious mind just waiting to be tapped. *Stilling the mind is the means by which we tap them.*

Happiness, however, is the *primary* thing we seek. The whole thrust of our existence is in the direction of happiness. Consciously or unconsciously, directly or indirectly, everything we have, everything we do and everything we are, is for one purpose only - to be happy. Our interest in education, marriage, raising children, earning more money, maintaining our health, advancing in our work - are all for the sake of happiness. The books we read, the clothes we buy, the places we go, the relationships we cultivate, the hobbies and entertainments we pursue, the religions and cultural traditions we practice, etc., all have happiness as their underlying motive.

But most of us have been ineffective in realizing happiness to anywhere near the degree possible. The reason is twofold: first, we are chasing what we already possess. Happiness is our case right now. It doesn't exist as a think to be sought after externally, but as an inherent potential to be realized from within. It is not something apart from us or alien to us, for as we have seen, bliss is who we are; it is our first name, our very nature and constitution. To chase after something we already possess is like a dog chasing its own tail - the more desperately he pursues it the more it eludes him and the more frustrated he becomes. We are in a state of happiness right now but do not realize it just as the dog already has his tail but doesn't realize it.

Happiness Is In The Pursuit

Some intelligent dogs, however, *do* realize they are chasing their own tails but do it just for the fun of it. For them, catching their tails is *not* the object of the game: *the object is the chase itself.* This is the second thing we're doing wrong - making the object more important than the chase. Happiness lies in the *pursuit* of an object or ideal, not in the *conquest* of it (the conquest is just a formality); for when the object is caught it means the end of the game. A cat, for example, lives only to catch a mouse, that is his greatest thrill in life, his whole reason for being. He spends most of his waking hours preparing and practicing for it. But when he finally does catch one, it is almost anticlimactic; he is immediately bored and will then try to prolong the chase by poking and prodding the mouse into fleeing again. But the mouse soon dies and the cat is left despondent knowing that the game is over. When the mouse died the cat effectively died too.

This principle that true happiness lies in the pursuit rather than in the conquest can be similarly observed when we lose an adversary or a loved one. When an adversary dies we don't usually feel relief, as might be expected, but rather a sense of personal loss. We had been at odds for so long, that our resentment had become a habit. We came to enjoy resenting that person; it became one of our chief pastimes. So when he dies or goes away we are not glad but feel an emptiness much like the cat whose mouse had died. We don't really miss the *person*, we miss the resenting (the pursuing), for if we have anger within us, one person is as good as another. The object of our resentment is secondary; the primary thing is the ongoing activity of resenting. And likewise when we lose a loved one: we don't really grieve the loss of the *person* himself but the loss of the *loving* (pursuing) of that person. Again, the *object* of our love is secondary to the loving itself. If we have love within us one person is as good as another. It is the loving itself that we enjoy, not the person; the person is just a medium.

Happiness, then, isn't found *in* people and things, but *through* them. It is a fine but crucial distinction. Our work and relationships are the field, medium, or means through which the happiness that is within, may be realized and expressed. Similarly, happiness is realized *through* listening to good music, seeing a colorful sunset, tasting a delicious apple, feeding a sparrow, smelling a rose, building a better can opener. Again, music is not important, but listening is; food is not the think, tasting is; flowers are not important, smelling is; a better can opener is not the essential thing, but being creative is. These "activities" serve to draw out the happiness that is latent within us; they simply act as spurs or catalyzing devices. A flower means nothing in and of itself; it is only when the color, form and fragrance of it agrees, harmonizes or relates to complementary qualities within us that we experience beauty and enjoyment.

Happiness Is A Creative Activity

What this all boils down to is that happiness isn't something that happens by accident but is a moment-to-moment, conscious, *creative activity*. To create means to discover, to draw out something that already exists. Happiness already exists to an unlimited degree. All that remains is for us to realize it more and more, to uncover it more and more.

Life itself has no purpose that needs to be fulfilled; it has already been purposed and fully filled. Life has nothing else to do but give and we have nothing else to do but partake; life is ever the lover and we are ever the beloved.

Life is a game whose object is to continually discover this inner happiness, this "most high" thing within us (and then to share it with others); everything else is secondary, superficial, and subordinate. You can call it finding freedom, finding your "self," finding God, truth, love, Christ, security, heaven, peace, reality - it doesn't matter what word or symbol you call it - they are all the same thing. What matters is what it is, what it means. The meaning of life is to realize it has no meaning; the goal of life is to realize it has no goal; the purpose of life is to realize it has no purpose. Life, consciousness, and bliss are all there is and all there has to be. It's only when we're *not* alive, *not* aware, and *not* happy that we have to invent purpose and meaning.

Before we go on to see how these three qualities are increased, let me just reiterate a few points: that happiness is indeed what we want in life regardless of how you translate the word at this particular time - for unless we are clear about our general, overall direction, we'll just waste time and energy; that happiness is an ongoing creative activity *not* an emotional one; that our errors have been seeking what we already possess, and making the destination more important than the journey.

The Intelligence Of The Organism

Notice now that of the three elements comprising the universal success formula, only *consciousness* is controllable. Life is fixed, and happiness is tied to consciousness - the more aware we are, the more happy; the less aware, the less happy. Consciousness is the only element we can do anything about; it's the only element that is manageable.

People come in various degrees of consciousness. Some of us just barely know we're alive, and a handful of us are 100 percent awake. But the masses of us are conscious to only about 15 percent of our possibilities. This means that only 15 percent of ourself has been realized. We are only 15 percent as alive, happy, and personally effective as we could be. The other 85 percent lies dormant in the subconscious mind. The subconscious part contains the balance of all the intelligence that makes up the total organism that we consist of. It contains the brilliant guidance system that led us, and continues to lead us, from darkness to consciousness. It is the organism that pumps our blood, digests our food, respirates our oxygen, and heals our wounds - even as we sleep. It is on constant alert twenty-four hours a day, never ceasing to watch out for us. It is an organism of exquisite perfection whose sole purpose is our beneficence. It is pure love, pure intelligence, and pure power, all rolled into one.

Accessing The Subconscious Mind

The way we tap, communicate with, or tune in to the subconscious part of the mind is by calming the conscious part. The conscious mind is constantly moving with thought, emotion, tension and distraction; the subconscious mind is still. The idea is to relax the conscious mind to the same degree as the subconscious mind. At that point, the information or intelligence from the one can transfer to the other. The process is like that of an airplane being refueled in mid-air by another. The transfer of fuel can only take place when both are moving at the exact same speed. Or think of the subconscious mind as a relaxed sewing needle and the conscious mind as a nervous length of thread. The thread must relax before it can pass through the eye of the needle.

We know that the universe is balanced; when the individual is balanced, he is then, in effect, one with the universe - that is, one with the subconscious. He and it are no longer separated, divided, conflicted, but are now in harmony, in alignment, in tune. The two are now related; they have come to union. Consequently, whatever intelligence is inherent in the organism or subconscious now becomes conscious, now comes into awareness. We realize our natural talents and abilities, make actual what was latent, awaken what was asleep, find what was lost.

The relationship between the conscious and subconscious minds can be compared with that between a radio receiver and transmitter. The transmitter is like the subconscious mind; it is where all the information or intelligence comes from; it is the *source*. And the receiver is like the conscious mind; its job is to be *receptive* to the source. It cannot be receptive, however, unless it's tuned in to the transmitter, and it cannot be tuned in to the transmitter unless the mind (the dial) is still. When we are excited, agitated, nervous, it is as if we are chaotically and indiscriminately spinning the dial back and forth without ever coming to a rest, and so receiving only jibberish as a result.

Or think of the conscious and subconscious minds as the two sections of an hourglass: the subconscious is the top half, and only 15 percent of it at a time can ever flow into consciousness, the bottom half. The narrow-minded neck restricts the flow. As we become open-minded through not taking life so personally, we, in effect, widen the neck of the hourglass until it looks like a water glass. Now, what is above can flow freely below; now they are equal or balanced; now there is no difference between the top and the bottom; now they are one, not two. There is no separation, no obstruction, no distinction. What is subconscious becomes directly and immediately conscious. The part returns to the whole as the river returns to the ocean and our intelligence and joy become revealed and expressed.

The Goal Of Human Evolution

The goal of human evolution is a movement away from *self*-consciousness toward balance or *situation*-consciousness. It is moving away from seeing things through our own narrow, personal perspective, to seeing things as they are, through a neutral or universal perspective. It is to view ourselves as an integral part of the situation or relationship we are in, instead of as an outsider looking in. We make a situation what it is and it makes us what we are. We are not separate from the situation (the universe) but are one with it. Remember from the last chapter that we just created the *illusion* of being separate or different in order to provide the contrast necessary to become self-conscious. The goal of growth, maturity, true education, and individual civilization is to now return to balance, to *un*self- consciousness. Our organism (universe) was and is perfect, but *artificially* became imperfect or imbalanced only to provide the impetus or stimulation necessary to begin "material" creation (for when you are perfect, you don't really *have* to *do* anything). Our tendency now is to heal, so to speak, to return to balance, wholeness, truth - only this time, not just as a living being, but as a fully conscious and happy one as well.

It's of course only natural that in order to become *un*-self-conscious we must first *be* self-conscious. A thing has to be known before it can be forgotten. Once you *know* something, you don't have to think about it any more; you rise above it. Once a child learns to walk he never gives it another thought. Walking has become "natural" and the mechanical details of it can be forgotten. The same applies to learning to ride a bicycle or operate a typewriter, in order to become *un*self-conscious about it, you first have to *be* self-conscious about it. In order to forget yourself there must first be a self to forget. And here is the problem - that you can't forget yourself until you find yourself, and you can't find yourself until you forget yourself. Relaxation (not thinking at all) resolves or transcends this paradox by returning you back to the center of balance, back to the "zero" point where both occur simultaneously. In this way you can express yourself to the fullest without being conscious of it in the slightest.

Controlling The Emotional Thermostat

Now higher consciousness (and its corresponding joy) do not necessarily come all at once, but only to the degree we can handle it without getting excited. That is the catch. Relaxation allows awareness to increase, but as soon as it does increase, excitement about it immediately blocks its continuance. So we move one step forward then one step backward, either not growing at all or growing at the pace of a snail. This up and down relaxation/excitement cycle works just like a thermostat control: consciousness (and joy) rises to the point of excitement - then shuts off. Our task becomes raising the excitement point higher and higher so that consciousness, intelligence, awareness, can rise without limitation. In other words, we want to become less and less excited about more and more things. Maturity, wisdom, composure is nothing more than the ability to either enjoy or suffer without making an emotional issue of it.

The Principle Of Creativity

The inspiration of the painter, poet, musical composer comes only when he is able to view his work with emotional detachment. He becomes tense when ideas do not flow and when they do, excitement prevents their sustainment. He suffers because what he clearly knows in his mind and feels in his heart will not translate faithfully onto a canvas or into words or music. He is blocked. Emotion has stifled his power of perception and expression. The creative genius in any medium is the one who has learned to overcome a restless mind and an anxious heart. He can maintain a serene indifference during both the creative feasts and famines alike; consequently, the famines occur less and less and the feasts, more and more.

The same principle of creative success that applies to the "artificial" artist applies to the "real" artist, the artist of living and being. Everyone is an artist, and his medium is his work or his role in a given relationship or situation. Non-emotional involvement in our work or role is the master key to achieving the outcome we desire.

Creativity Needs A Specific Goal

Creatively "achieving the outcome we desire" implies having a *particular* goal in mind. Happiness is the general goal but we need to be more specific than that. Only when our goal is clear or our problem is identified can the creative juices begin to flow.

Creative power is nothing more than discriminating power. It is the ability to see what is significant with respect to our goal among that which appears on the surface to be insignificant. This power is based on the understanding that there is nothing really irrelevant in our experience. Every situation, every encounter, however trivial it may outwardly seem, contains something meaningful and beneficial with respect to our problems, questions, growth or goals; for in a universe where everything is related on some level to everything else, all we need do is open our blinders a little wider to see how this moment directly or indirectly relates to it. When we are in step with the world we can see, as Aristotle put it, "the correspondences between things." We can put "two and two" together; we can see how two seemingly unconnected things are indeed connected.

This, for example, is how "accidental" scientific discoveries are made. Newton gained insight into the laws of gravity when an apple fell on his head; penicillin was discovered when mold on bread was found to "eat" bacteria; Gutenburg creatively put together a wine press and an engraving of a royal seal to discover the printing press, and so on. Discoveries such as these happen in the particular area a person is working. Newton didn't notice the relationship between a wine press and an engraving because he wasn't working in that direction, and likewise with the others. Positive "accidents" or "good luck" happen to those who are receptive or tuned to a *par-*

ticular direction. Columbus didn't discover America by bobbing along at random, he maintained a firm westerly direction. And likewise if channel three is your goal you point your antennae in that direction and receive out of the crowded atmosphere only those signals relating to channel three.

So where the first rule of creative power is emotional detachment, the second rule is to have a particular goal, purpose, or question in mind - for if we don't know *specifically* where we're going, getting there will be very difficult.

Ideas, goals, games, and purposes come from noticing where improvements can be made in the quality of your life or the lives of others and then doing something about it. They come from noticing what is missing, ineffective, inefficient or imbalanced and then proceeding to fill the void or right the wrong. They come from noticing what is not working in your financial life, love life, spiritual life, intellectual life and then taking action to correct it.

The Principle Of "Already Being There"

The third step in the creative process, besides being detached and specific, is *knowing* in your mind and heart that you *can* do it. And then the fourth and final step is to just go ahead and do it.

Let's say you have some clear goal or task in mind, the next step is to *assume you've already arrived*. You know where you're heading, now you want to mentally "already be there." This will entail anticipating the steps necessary to getting there. These steps would constitute your plan. A goal is *what* you want; a plan is *how* you achieve it.

Let's say your goal is to bake a cake. First, you must be specific. You can't bake "a" cake but must have a *particular* one in mind - a chocolate-layer cake, for instance. In your mind, the cake is not "already" done because some questions spring up like, "What is the recipe? Do I have the ingredients? Do I have the necessary utensils and baking equipment?" Once these questions have been affirmatively answered, in your mind the cake is already done; it's as good as baked and all you have to do is go through the motions. The common sense questions gave you your plan: (1) have the recipe; (2) have the ingredients; (3) have the oven. That done, you now have faith the cake will be done. The cake is not actually baked, but you *know* it will be. This "knowing" is prerequisite to successful accomplishment. If you only think, believe, guess, or hope you can do it then you will not do it. "Thinking" as opposed to "knowing" indicates you are missing one of the key ingredients and are not aware of it. It means you haven't asked the right questions. The master question to always ask is this: "*What specifically is separating me from already being at my goal?*" Keep answering this question until, in your mind, you know you are there. A question always indicates that you do not yet know what you're doing. When there are no more questions - you are there.

The creative process, then, went like this: you saw an empty cake pan (or an empty canvas if you were a painter, an empty sheet of paper if you were a writer, an empty cash register if you were a businessperson, etc.), conceived through emotional detachment of how it could be filled, knew by asking the appropriate questions that it could be done and then went ahead and did it by putting one foot in front of the other. You took what was merely an idea in your head and converted it to something real, something substantial. You took an idea and made it flesh. You took a *conception* of a cake and made it an *actual* cake. First there was nothing and then there was something. First there was an empty cake pan and presto - it was full. An act of creation.

The cake was delicious but you can no longer see your feet, so you decide to lose some weight. Again, you must be specific about your goal: exactly how much weight do you want to lose and by when do you want to lose it? You are overweight by twelve pounds and wish to lose them over a one month period. This translates to 6.4

ounces per day or about 200 calories. In your mind you have not "already" lost the weight because some questions emerge. "What specific way can 200 calories per day be dropped from my usual diet? Shall I cut portion sizes? From how much to how much? Can I substitute fattening items for less fattening ones? Which ones? How much of this reduction can be accomplished through physical exercise? Which exercise? Where, when and for how many minutes a day will I do it?" Once these questions are answered to your satisfaction you can relax and consider yourself "already" at your desired weight. All that remains is for the month to pass.

As a final example, let's say you desire to take an automobile trip from Los Angeles to Boston. You are not "already" there because some questions arise: "Is the car in good enough condition to make the trip? How are the tires? Which route will I travel?" Do I have enough money? What clothes will I bring and where will I stay on arrival?" etc. Once such questions are resolved you can consider yourself as practically being there. The actual driving part becomes a mere formality. In your mind you are "already" in Boston. Any obstacles that pop up along the way to your goal such as "No Vacancy" signs, flat tires and detours, are taken in stride as a routine part of the creative process.

The only difference between where you are now and where you want to be is just time and space. Before we had a body life was much simpler. If we wanted to create a cake, we just had to imagine there was a cake and immediately there would be one. There were no time and space restrictions. We didn't have to go through all the motions of shopping, mixing and baking; all we had to do was say the word - "Let there be a chocolate-layer cake" and there it would be. Our thought waves would stir the ethers into whatever form we chose. But since we have grown so physical and sluggish the whole creative process has been stretched out like a movie in slow-motion. It remains the same in the sense that we can still create "something" out of "nothing" but instead of just "saying the word" we must now go through all the motions as well; we must enter into physical activity.

Notice that by merely becoming more and more specific about your goals or problems they tend to solve themselves. Problem solving is nothing more than the process of becoming more and more specific until the solution finally occurs to you. You began with vague, general ideas to bake a cake, lose some weight, drive to Boston. And as you became more specific about them, you simultaneously evolved plans to achieve them. Notice also that becoming more specific about your problems and desires naturally involved the process of converting them into questions. This seems obvious. If an answer is what you seek then a question is what you ask. There cannot be an answer without a question. But what is less obvious and more important is that the reverse is also true: *you cannot have a question without an answer*. This means that if you have the question within you then you must also have the answer within you as well. It cannot be otherwise for they are two halves of the same coin. The question could not be formed at all if in the subconscious mind there was not already the answer. The answer is the background from which the question must come. A question, then, is proof positive that the answer already exists within us, for like a scene in a picture, the foreground cannot be noticed unless by contrast with the background. The background is exactly what makes the foreground come forward - the answer is exactly what makes the question come forward.

The key to tapping the subconscious mind, then, lies first in formulating the question and then simply being still and receptive to the answer "Shall I take this course of action (or not)?" "Is this the time to sell (or buy)?" A question works as a differentiating device much like a radio tuner that separates the stations you want from those you don't want, or like a fog light that slices through all the noise and confusion to focus exactly where you want it to. Once you have the question clearly articulated the problem is half, if not completely solved; for it often happens that the answer is spontaneously triggered in the very process of articulating the question. Otherwise the answer may come to you in a few hours, days, weeks, or longer depending on the complexity of the problem. If you do not have a clear question and are just generally perplexed about a situation, then simply acknowledge that that's the case and leave *that* as your question.

Answers may come when you least expect them. You may be shopping, showering, or in the middle of a deep sleep. The trick is not to push or strain for the answer for that will only push it further back. The mind, like a cat or a child, does not respond to force or pressure but only to persistent calmness and patience.

When we remain composed problems tend to unravel themselves. A problem is like a knot we have to untie; when tense and impatient we tend to pull at it blindly and make it tighter. But when relaxed, we can see *how* the knot is intertwined so that taking it apart becomes routine. A problem is like driving over a hill and seeing miles of curved and hilly road ahead, but as you proceed, the hills tend to flatten out and the curves unravel before you. What *appear* to be sharp curves and steep hills from a distance turn out to be slow curves and only gradual inclines when you actually get there; you barely have to move the steering wheel or increase acceleration.

Imitating Success

A third thing to notice in these examples of how the creative process is structured is the fact that in all three cases you copied someone else's success. This is not just convenient, it is a universal law: you cannot create anything that doesn't already exist on some level. Whatever your goal is, its accomplishment will always be an extension of either your previous success or that of someone else. Your success in baking that cake was based on someone else's recipe. Someone before you perfected it and you simply duplicated it. The same with diet programs. Someone discovers an effective way to lose weight,we copy it and similarly benefit. And likewise when driving cross- country, the route you traveled was mapped out by others before you - you copied someone else's route. Thus the most efficient way to get from point A to point B, is not to re-invent the wheel, but to copy someone who has already done it effectively.

First, look within your own area of expertise or interest for a successful businessperson, artist, product, service, company, or idea to use as a model. The creative part is then to improve on it. First imitate, then innovate. Simply duplicating it does not work; you must do it better, faster, or less expensively. Copying a successful ice cream operation is not enough; you must then improve on it by offering chocolate sprinkles or flavored cones at no extra charge, for example.

In observing that which is successful, you are to look at *what* is being done and *how* it is being done. "What" and "how"; those are the two questions that will lead you to the essence of the thing. "Why" questions are irrelevant and academic. A thing is successful for the same reason that the grass is green - because that's the way it is. In school, you ask "why"; in the field, you ask "what" and "how".

The idea is to discover a thing's structure or technique and then adapt it to your own personality. You don't want to change the structure of the thing, only the contents. You don't want to throw away the cup, just change the flavor of the contents. For instance, in improving that chocolate cake, you might substitute natural honey for processed sugar; in a new diet program you might replace all the meat dishes with fish dishes; in that cross-country trip, you might discover a route that is not only fast but that has cultural or scenic value as well. Thus you've created an original recipe for chocolate cake, a new diet program, and a new travel guide. If you want to know how to promote these things find a successful promoter and copy him. If you want to write books on these subjects, find successful ones and copy their format, etc.

Life Is A Recreational Activity

Since life has no goal or purpose of its own, any that we set up will be purely recreational and may be thought of as a "game." A game or goal serves first, as a medium through which to realize happiness on the spiritual level, and second, to realize prosperity on the material level. I specify first and second because just as higher consciousness must precede happiness, so happiness must come before prosperity. Prosperity is first a state of mind and second, a state of pocketbook. The common misconception is that prosperity brings happiness but just the reverse is true - happiness brings prosperity; for unless you are calm and content to begin with, the creative power necessary to prosper will be limited. This principle assumes, of course, that being successful and not being happy, is not being successful, and being successful at the cost of ulcers and heart disease is also not being successful.

The word *game* implies something that is not to be taken morbidly or seriously, for seriousness is itself a dis-ease. It indicates we are taking the game personally, taking for real what is only artificial. Any violation of reality or balance will cause dis-ease, and seriousness violates the reality that the games of life are artibrary and recreational. They have no intrinsic value of their own; their value is artifically and externally placed on them for conventional purposes. A diamond jewel, for instance, has relatively little value in and of itself. It is simply a hard piece of crystal cut to shine better. Both its symbolic and monetary values are placed on it externally.

That the activities of life are not to be taken seriously does not mean one is not to participate in them firmly, fully and with total dedication and resoluteness. There is a vast difference between being serious about your game and involving yourself in it wholeheartedly. Seriousness means you are personally identifying with the game instead of creatively identifying with it; you are mistakenly treating the game as though it were a real extension of you rather than a superficial extension of you. To participate 100 percent in a thing, and at the same time be in accord with the law of balance - one must work for the sake of the work itself, for the sake of the game itself. The successful person does not work for personal glory but for the glory of the game, for the glory of the action. Only when you see the game as being detached from you as a person are you free to participate in it with your whole being. Once the ego is removed from the picture, all fear is removed as well, and when all fear is removed nothing remains to inhibit full self- expression. There are no fears as to whether you will win or lose for you'll see that the outcome of the game is secondary to playing it to the fullest which is primary. If you have one eye on the score you will only have one eye left to play the game with. Thoughts of success or failure are emotional or ego activities and have no relevance to reality. In the real world failure is impossible; in the egotistical world success is impossible.

Not participating fully in a thing is a common defense mechanism the ego uses to protect itself against the *imagination* of failure. By withholding full expression of ourselves we have convenient justification if the outcome is not favorable. The catch, of course, is that with this policy, it never will be favorable for "a turtle never gets anywhere without sticking its [egotistical] head out."

There is no more anxiety or stress, for now you know what you are doing, why you are doing it, and how you are doing it. You don't stray from your plan by thinking, saying, or doing anything that does not relate to that plan in some way. You know that love, happiness, joy is the name of the game and the foundation and motivation for all that you do. You now participate 100 percent in all your activities and relationships holding nothing of yourself back. You are now in tune with reality and everything now works in your favor. Ideas and opportunities will bombard you from every direction. You will routinely find yourself in the right place at the right time. Open a book at random and that page will just happen to contain the information you've been seeking;

traffic lights will just happen to turn green as you approach; what is in your best interest will just happen to coincide with the best interests of those you come into contact with along the way, and so on.

As your general awareness of life increases, a loving happiness will become your natural response; worldly wisdom is a consequence of world awareness. The combination of worldly wisdom plus a loving happiness results in creative power in the form of personal effectiveness. Your power will come from being simply and unpretensiously who you are. By being unaffected you will affect everyone; by not needing to impress anyone you will impress everyone. Your composure will be assuring, your enthusiasm will be contagious, your cheerfulness will be infectious and your sensitivity, delightful.

PART TWO

THE PROCESS OF BECOMING MENTALLY FREE

CHAPTER 4

CONTROLLING PAIN AND PLEASURE

Pain is Overcome by Indifference to Superficial Extremes

Contentedness means that if all your goals and desires were never to be fulfilled or realized it wouldn't make the slightest difference to your happiness or well-being. If it doesn't make any difference whether or not you attain, you have already attained; if it doesn't make any difference whether or not you win, you have already won. This is a universal law and this is what being relaxed and objective is.

Whatever you want in life you must come from the spirit that you *already* have it. Whether your desires are material, intellectual or spiritual, to find contentment, security and fulfillment in the future you must be content, secure and fulfilled *now*.

To be relaxed means you are no longer in need or want. You are no longer deficient or lacking in anything. Nothing is missing from you. You are now complete and whole. You have reached to the understanding that all things are just as they are supposed to be. You have arrived. Whether you are a machine operator, a board chairman, or a housewife, it is only calmness and contentment that indicates you have succeeded in life, that you have overcome the world, that you are free and secure.

Contentedness is indifference to both pleasure and pain. As far as the contented person is concerned, they are both the same; he is unchanged by either. If something happens to be pleasing, that is nice; if it happens to be wrong or unpleasant, that is too bad. Either way he is not affected, but remains himself - calm, clear, satisfied.

Indifference means you are satisfied with what is, with whatever happens to be at the moment. You don't desire that a situation be different than it is in order for you to be satisfied, for you're satisfied with whatever is.

The opposite of indifference is *desire*. When we desire pleasure and gratification, it means we have left the state of balance and contentment, and emotional pain will be the inevitable result. There is nothing wrong, of course, with pleasure and gratification in and of themselves, it is the *desiring* part of the equation that causes all the mischief. Desiring is the emotional force that pulls us off balance and into the negative cause and effect whirlpool. Craving gratification is an emotional activity, and just like a physical activity it is subject to the law of reverse effort which says that "All action produces an equal and opposite reaction." So that whenever we seek after pleasure we always get the opposite - pain.

This principle also applies if we are experiencing pleasure right now and try to cling to it. The clinging, like the desiring, causes the pleasure to change to pain. But if we are experiencing pleasure and are indifferent to it - it remains. And the same is true of emotional pain - if we try to escape it, it persists, but if we experience it totally and indifferently, it changes to pleasure.

Pleasure is relaxation and enjoyment. It indicates physical and emotional balance. Physical balance is the absence of physical pain and emotional balance is the absence of emotional pain such as anxiety or discontent. When you have no aches or desires you are happy. Being without pain and being happy is natural. The proof that it is natural lies in the fact that when we are without pain we do not notice it, but if we have a headache, a worry, or a desire, we are continuously uneasy. Pleasure is the norm, and pain, the aberration. When there is no pain we just happily go about our business without thinking about it. To be delighted does not need a reason, but to suffer you need a toothache, a guilt complex, or more and more money, excitement or power, etc.

Needing a reason to be happy is not natural; it indicates dis-ease. If you need a *reason* to be happy then you can never be happy because the illusory deficiency or imbalance that seeks for a reason now will remain with you always. As soon as you are about to meet your criteria for happiness immediately your imbalance will pop up with yet another requirement, and then another. Your work is never rewarding enough; life is never stimulating enough; you never meet the "right" man or woman; you never have the money, possessions or security that you think you need; you never receive enough appreciation or recognition, etc. Imbalance endlessly breeds further imbalance. It is like trying to stabilize a rocking canoe, as soon as you move to one side, immediately the other side wants to tip you. Once you start looking for a reason to be happy you will *always* be looking. Nothing will satisfy you. Everything will contain some insufficiency, some defect. Something will always be missing or falling just short of the mark.

If you are not content with what *is*, with what is the situation at this very moment, then you cannot be content with what should, would, or could be either. What *is*, is real; what *should be* is fantasy. Living in reality, in and of itself regardless of contents, is pleasing and gratifying; but living in fantasy, living in accordance with how things should be, breeds endless frustration. If you are not happy in the rain, you cannot be happy in the sun either for they are two sides of the same coin. In the first place, you cannot accept or reject only half a coin, and in the second place, the whole coin is irrelevant to happiness. Happiness is not dependent on circumstances; it is totally self-sufficient. It needs no politics, religion, science or philosophy. It does not come *from* things but exists in and of itself. Nothing external is needed. Happiness is just the way life is whether we like it or not and has nothing to do with rain or shine, good or bad, right or wrong. Circumstances are just the props of life, just the scenery, setting or background material. The backdrop is always changing, but the real you, the authentic you, always remains the same. One day you wear a blue suit, the next day a gray one; one day goes well, the next day doesn't. Behind the suit and aside from the fluctuations in the market, you are the very same person. The real you cannot change, cannot become unhappy. Unhappiness is a dis-ease that doesn't occur in nature; it is something that is acquired, and we acquire it through desiring that things be different than what they are right now. Life is neutral; it becomes a problem when we judge and criticize it, and becomes a pleasure when we view it indifferently.

Pain Is An Imbalance Warning Signal

The purpose of physical and emotional pain is to warn us that we're doing something unhealthy. In health, the whole organism is working harmoniously; in disease, some imbalance or conflict has occured and physical or emotional pain is the means by which we are informed of it. If you are sitting on a hot stove the pain would alert you of the danger otherwise you would fry to death and not even know it. And the same is true of emotional pain such as that of anxiety or resentment; it is to remind us we are thinking or desiring something inappropriate - such as killing the person who turned the stove on.

So pain is a positive thing; it is a friend not an enemy. It is not the problem itself but merely the messenger.

Our mistake, of course, is that we try to kill the messenger instead of the *cause* of the problem. When there is physical pain we respond quickly and decisively. We notice what is causing the pain and immediately act on it. As soon as we notice the stove is hot we jump off and are not likely to repeat the same mistake twice. But emotional pain and tension are more subtle, not so great an emergency. So instead of seeing and admitting we are doing something wrong, we try to kill the messenger with various drugs and distractions. We, and conventional medical practice, treat the symptoms not the cause so that relief, if there is any, is only superficial and temporary. It is like instead of getting off the hot stove you just stood there taking aspirins and tranquilizers.

The implication of all this is that maintaining a balanced perspective is not a choice but a *law*. The universe is so structured that if we do not maintain an attitude of contented indifference toward people and things we will get burnt by pain and dis-ease.

Success is finding your own level, your own place. It is not to go too fast or be too ambitious, and it is not to go too slow or be stagnant; it is to remain directly in the middle. The world turns at a certain speed and it is for you to find that speed. Pain and tension will be your foolproof guide. Simply notice what you are doing at the moment tension arises, and then stop doing it. No need to rationalize it or intellectualize it; simply notice the tension, notice what you are doing at the time, and then stop doing it. When Pinocchio lied his nose grew; when we lie against our nature, tension grows.

Crying For The Moon

Tension comes from either desiring something you already have, as we discussed earlier, or desiring something you cannot have. Let's say you are walking down the street and in a shop window see the most beautiful watch. You desire to own it but can't afford it. Notice the word "but" in this example. This "but" is the key to anxiety; it is what creates the conflict. Just as the "but" splits the sentence in two, it also splits the mind in two. If you could afford that watch you wouldn't desire it; you would simply buy it! You would see it, like it and buy it. No "buts" about it and no conflict or stress involved. The secret of contentment, then, is this: if you can have a thing, have it, but if you cannot - don't desire it. In other words, don't desire what is not already yours.

You can, however, create what is not yours. If you would have that watch then make it a creative activity instead of an emotional one. To desire is emotional; to create is spiritual. Use the creative strategy outlined earlier to convert the idea of possessing that watch into actually possessing it.

Longing for anything is incompatible with reality because your organism already knows what all your needs and desires are and is already working toward their attainment. Whether you are aware of it or not you are always heading in the direction of total fulfillment. The key is to just be more aware and receptive. All things being equal, health, happiness and abundance are already your case; they are already programmed into your genes. The whole task of intelligence is to just keep "all things equal," to just get out of the way and let nature run its course, to just follow the leading of common sense, and to not ignore it when tension reminds you that you've stepped out of line.

We are the only hindrance to success. By desiring, we effectively contradict our own self, our own organism. It is like turning on the car's starter while the engine is already running, or driving with the emergency brake on. How frustrating and self-defeating.

It's even incorrect to desire "natural" things such as food and sex. When you are hungry, eat, when sex is appropriate, then have sex. No desiring is involved. When you crave food in between meals you are not relaxed and are using food as a drug rather than as a source of nutrition. And likewise with sex; if you are desiring sex in between sexual meals then you are either using sex as a drug or you have been suppressing it. Many of us have been conditioned to view sex in a narrow way, in which case, it will consume a large part of our head. If someone says, "Don't think about elephants," then, by the law or reverse effort, elephants are all we will think about. Eating and sex are not emotional activities but are creative or recreational ones. They are not to be hankered after, suppressed or abused, but are to be enjoyed and appreciated in their season.

The Law Of Reverse Effort

Emotional activity brings about the opposite of what we want according to the same principle that propels a rocket or a jet airplane. In a balanced universe, movement one way must be compensated for by an equivalent movement the opposite way in order to maintain the balance. The force of a plane's engine in one direction causes the plane to react in the opposite direction. So to make the plane go east we must aim the energy toward the west. If we want the rocket to go *up*, we aim the energy *down*. And in the same way, if we want pain and tension we exert energy towards pleasure and gratification.

But we cannot apply this principle in reverse as the masochist attempts to do. We cannot say, "I will then seek pain in order to find pleasure." This does not work either, for seeking pain is just as unreal as seeking pleasure. Again, the problem is not *what* you seek but is *that* you seek. The world turns in only one direction and that direction is neutral. If happiness is what you want, then neutrality is your direction.

As another example of this law of reverse effort, think of a revolving door as the world. The door in front of you is "pleasure" and the one behind you is "pain." When you push towards pleasure, pain comes right on your heels. Now let's say the doors are in motion. Perhaps there is someone in the compartment in front of you and someone in the one behind you, and they are doing all the pushing. All you have to do now is just enjoy the ride. You do not have to push for pleasure but just remain neutral by moving at the same speed the doors (the world) are moving.

This is a good example of creative movement where you are still while at the same time in action. You are moving but are still with respect to the doors. As far as the doors are concerned you are not moving at all. The world is moving and you are moving with it. You are in unison. You and the world are not moving in different directions or different speeds but are equal in all respects.

A See-Saw Named Desire

Imagine the world is a child's see-saw, half of which is "pleasure," half is "pain," and you are situated exactly at the center. The see-saw is in perfect balance; that is, until you begin to step out in the direction of "pleasure" causing it to fall and "pain" to simultaneously rise up and become dominant.

To desire is like trying to remove a speck from your soup. As you approach it with your spoon, it slips away, and the faster you chase it, the faster it moves in the opposite direction. The only way to catch it is to chase it creatively rather than emotionally. That is to say, instead of *moving* after it, be *still* and let it come to you. Hold the spoon just below the surface of the soup in such a way that the speck falls into the spoon naturally, by gravity. Thus you catch it without chasing it.

The reason the speck eludes the spoon so naturally is because they are physically connected to each other so have no choice. The soup is what connects them together. The soup, however fluid it may be, is the physical link that keeps them separate. Just as a car and its trailer stay separate by virtue of the hitch between them, so the spoon and speck stay separate by virtue of the soup between them. And the way it works physically is the way it works emotionally: Pain and pleasure are directly linked together but we don't notice the connection between them because it's so subtle in the same way that we don't notice the soup as a connective because it is so soupy.

Thus pain and pleasure are connected together as two sides of one continuous coin. If we move toward pleasure we come to pain, and if we move away from pain, it follows us. Our only alternative is to transcend the whole coin, to rise above the entire issue. We do this by moving on the edge or center of the coin instead of on either surface of it. By remaining at the center, the point of indifference, we experience *natural* pleasure *all* of the time instead of *emotional* pleasure *some* of the time.

Clinging To Pleasure Changes It To Pain

If we are experiencing pleasure at the moment and try to hold on to it, we lose it. Just as *effort* towards pleasure causes pain, so *effort* to keep the pleasure we are experiencing now also causes pain. Clinging to anything is, in effect, an attempt to control reality. But reality cannot be controlled because change is its very nature. A person finding a slice of chocolate cake delicious and gratifying would like to keep that gratification going, so he has another slice. But the second slice is not quite as good as the first, and the third is about to make him vomit. What was delicious a few slices ago has become a toxin, a poison. Clinging caused what was sweet to turn sour, not because the *cake* had changed each time, but because the *situation* had changed each time.

Or similarly, a person is enjoying sex and it is particularly beautiful. He would like to keep that feeling, so he has sex again three minutes later to try to duplicate the experience - but guess what? The second time is not as good; and with each subsequent attempt gets progressively less satisfying to the point where he never wants to have anything to do with sex again. Here as above, efforts to cling to something beautiful cause it to become the opposite, not because the physical sex act itself was different, but because the dynamics of the situation were different.

Each moment is different and unique. We are not the same person we were a moment ago and, if alive, will not be the same person a moment from now either. The experience of this moment will change us so that we will act and respond in a new and different way in the next moment. There is no "good" experience and no "bad" experience, only *different* experiences. The nature of reality is constant change and growth. Change is the only thing in life that is permanent. Heraclitus said, "You cannot step in the same river twice." To cling to past pleasures is a denial of life, growth and reality in the present moment. Each moment is a different snowflake, a different miracle. Carbon copies cannot exist among that which is alive but only with things that are dead. Only the dead are the same yesterday, today and tomorrow; the living are always moving, growing, creating.

The person who clings to life keeps missing it. Or in the words of the master of relaxation, "Whosoever would save his life shall lose it." The person who clings to the past is like a cartoon character working on an assembly line in a bottling plant. If he spends too long on the present bottle the next one crashes to the floor; and when he tries to save it the next one falls, and while trying to grab that one the next is lost and then the next, and so on.

We cannot cling to life because it is happening too fast, and we cannot escape from it either because we are surrounded by it. The only choice remaining is to let go and flow along with it, to be indifferent to it. And in that indifference lies precisely the relaxation and enjoyment we had been searching for all along. When the dog finally becomes frustrated and exhausted enough from chasing his own tail he lies down to rest only to discover his tail brushing against his lips.

Indifference to Pleasure Causes it to Remain

If you can experience pleasure without being affected by it then pleasure can never leave you. To understand how this happens you must first remember that joy is your normal, natural state of being so is nothing to get excited about. When you don't get excited about it you are then simply being yourself - happy. When there is contentment your mind is still like a placid lake. But as soon as you get excited it begins to move, to ripple; it's no longer still but agitated. Now it's different than it was; it was still but your emotional response changed it. So by remaining unmoved by pleasure the pleasure doesn't move either.

Escaping From Pain Causes It To Persist

Running away from pain doesn't work for the same reason chasing after gratification doesn't work - they are both emotional activities and anything emotional must, by law, backfire. Desiring is an emotional action, escaping is an emotional *re*action. They are equally negative in effect. In desire we get the opposite of what we want; in escape we get more of what we're escaping from. This principle can be seen in the same "revolving door" illustration used earlier. There we saw that in pushing "pleasure" we caused "pain" to move upon us. Here, by pushing the front door forward in order to escape the "pain" door behind us, we find the "pain" door follows us like a shadow. The actions in both cases are exactly the same only the motives are different. And both are doomed to failure, again, not because their motives are right or wrong but only because both are emotional.

Whatever we try to escape, avoid, resist or supress we give power to. Emotional pain has no power in and of itself to harm us, it is merely a signaling device, an indicator, a messenger. By avoiding the messenger we, in effect, make the messenger the issue instead of the imbalance it represents. The messenger then mistakenly becomes the evil to be dealt with. *It* becomes what we must resist, struggle with and kill. *It* is what we must drown with alcohol, screen with drugs, stuff with carbohydrates and distract with excitement.

But error is insatiable; it is a bottomless pit. When we attempt to treat the symptoms rather than the cause, nothing works. But the ego is stubborn and foolish; it doesn't want to see and admit that it's wrong, that it's selfish perspective is a false one. So it spends its life either avoiding the truth or trying to prove that a lie is the truth.

In this we see the basic difference between the creative and the emotional: the creative lives in truth, the emotional lives in fantasy; the creative is at ease, the emotional is disturbed; the creative comes from contentment, the emotional comes from hunger.

Experiencing Pain Changes It To Pleasure

The natural remedy for relaxing tension is simply to experience it fully and indifferently. To the degree tension is experienced rather than avoided, it disappears. The energy that goes into the act of experiencing is the same energy that reverses the tension, and at the same time, corrects the imbalance that brought the tension about. This is a most crucial point to understand. The energy that we experience with is not emotional but is still and passive. Notice now that we are eliminating the tension by contradicting it out of existence: Tension is emotion and movement, and experiencing is still and passive. It is impossible for the two to exist simultaneously so the tension is forced to relax or dissipate.

When we are experiencing tension without desiring that it should go away and without attempting to escape from it, we are then in a state of balance or indifference. In this state there is no movement, and where there is no movement there can be no tension. So tension becomes obsolete merely through the indifferent experiencing of it. In other words, to eliminate anything negative or unpleasant we move *into* it not away from it. Pain and pleasure are a continuum; they are one surface like the inside of the cup that continues to the outside of the cup. By entering into the pain we must eventually come to the pleasure just as by entering far enough into the night the day must appear. As night becomes day so pain becomes pleasure.

If you were feeling depressed, for instance, you would do nothing about it except to watch it indifferently. You would not like it, hate it, want it to stay or want it to leave but would impartially observe it out of existence.

Whenever there is any discomfort, whether it be from boredom, guilt, worry, resentment, anxiousness, depression, etc. just allow it to happen. Do not interfere with it in any way but just let it be itself. The negativity came through emotional involvement in the first place; to reverse the process we don't want to feed it more of the same. To reverse the process our involvement must become passive.

Pain is both a penalty and a teacher. The word *pain* comes from the Greek and Latin words meaning *penalty*. Pain is the penalty we pay for violating the law of balance. Pain is also a teacher in the sense that each time pain is experienced we would learn a lesson. Now truth is the most subtle thing in existence; it cannot pass through skulls that are too thick. So the thicker or more stubborn the skull the more suffering will be necessary in order to learn a particular lesson. And the principal lesson, again, is this: that the universe is balanced and indifferent so it is for us to be likewise; and if we are not, pain and tension will be the swift and sure penalty.

Appreciating Your Suffering

Contentment is appreciating your suffering knowing that its sole purpose is to lead you back to the truth which would free you from it. To appreciate a thing is to fully experience it. Each bit of discomfort that you experience to the end will leave you forever. The effects are cumulative so that a day comes when not a speck of it remains. Whenever nervousness or depression strike, do not be averse to it but enter into it, relish it as an opportunity to regain another bit of lost freedom. Look it straight in the eye with firmness, calmness and impartialness and watch it dissipate. Passive or creative energy works like a light that makes the dark disappear. As darkness is merely the absence of light so pain is merely the absence of awareness. By shining impartial attention on pain, its nothingness, its insubstantialness become exposed.

Contentment is the total acceptance of what others are or are not and whatever you are or are not. There are over four billion personalities in the world all seeing the world in a slightly different way. We can either relate to them all or relate to no one. The only way we can relate to them all is to accept them all just as they are. And likewise, we must accept ourselves in our totality. We are just as complex as the world is, the product of countless generations of evolutionary development. Everything we ever were is within us and everything we shall ever become is also within us. We consist of so many conflicting thoughts, feelings, attitudes and beliefs that the only way to relate to them all is to indifferently accept them all. If you are feeling jealousy, sadness, resentment, hate, greed, etc., accept it totally and completely. At those moments that is exactly who you are. To deny with guilt, regret or to give excuses and justification is a denial of yourself; it is a denial of truth, and pain and tension will be the inevitable upshot. When you are feeling angry, then be angry totally but with full awareness. Let it all out. Withhold nothing of your anger for whatever you hold back will fester in the form of resentment and poison your whole being. You will carry it around with you to negatively color all that you say, think, feel and do.

Now when you are totally acceptant and aware of your anger, that is, when you know you are free to fully feel and express it, an interesting thing happens - you don't get angry anymore. Anger is an explosive thing; it can only come when feelings have been repressed like gunpowder. Without repression there can be no explosion, they are two sides of the same coin. So an angry, resentful person is always a repressed person. He does not accept what he is and does not express what he is. And since he cannot accept himself it follows that he will not be able to accept anyone else either. If you are seeing defects in yourself you will be seeing defects in everyone, and whatever defect that you do see in another is exactly the defect you yourself possess in that moment. It is impossible to see a fault in another unless you also possess it, for as any child will tell you, "It takes one to know one."

Creating Your Own Monsters

If you desire to be successful then you must also desire to fail. It cannot be otherwise for again, they are two sides of the same coin. If you would be happy or successful, then *be* it! Why must you bring *desire* into the picture? By desiring you introduce a conflict into the situation that does not exist; you make struggle a foregone conclusion before even beginning; you create resistance merely by anticipating it; you create an adversary relationship between you and your goals that is imaginary. Your goals don't care if they are attained by you or not. They are totally indifferent to your designs on them. They are just sitting there to be partaken of or not to be partaken of. By desiring you put them on a pedestal and give them a prominence that is artificial. And the greater the desire the greater the prominence. You set yourself up to fail by creating blocks where none exist. For every desire there *must* also be a complementary block built into it. If there were no block there would be no desire, and if there is no desire there will be no block.

In reality you cannot desire and you cannot try; you either have it or you don't. The only question to ask yourself, then, is whether or not you have it. If not, no amount of desire and effort will help. A flower does not desire to grow and does not use effort; it simply grows. It has a purpose but not an ego. An ego is emotional while a purpose is creative. The purpose of a flower is to flower. And its source of power is the sun. Now all it has to do is let go and be itself in the direction of its source, and creation happens of its own accord. No desire, effort or ego ambition is involved. It is just being itself, and to just *be* is automatically to flower. It just relaxes, and out of that stillness, out of that "holy indifference" it joyously blooms into the richest colors and the sweetest perfumes.

CHAPTER 5

BECOMING DEPROGRAMMED

Preformed Opinions Inhibit Self-Expression

Relaxation is achieved by letting go of all preconceptions you hold about life, and living spontaneously by common sense. By "preconceptions" I mean any fixed ideas, beliefs, attitudes or judgments as to what is true or false, right or wrong, good or bad, possible or impossible.

Spontaneity is living in accordance with how things *are*, not with how you *think* they are. You cannot *know* how things are if your head is filled with preconceptions of how they are. Thinking takes time and life is happening and changing too fast. In order to be sensitive and receptive to the ever-changing newness of it, the old must continually and instantaneously be let go. We cannot write on a chalkboard that's filled with yesterdays' scribblings; it must be erased first, otherwise the past will not only influence, affect, and interfere with the present, but will *prevent* the present as well.

Spontaneity is direct and immediate knowing, acting, and responding. It is a state of total flexibility and open-mindedness where there is no time or space between what is happening and a response that is appropriate to it. You are connected to the moment as directly and harmoniously as a dancer is to his partner. When he moves forward, she simultaneously moves backward, and vice versa. Their movements are not thought about or premeditated, and exactly *because* they are not, a perfect synchrony is automatically and effortlessly maintained.

To live from the past is like suffering a permanent hangover. When we eat or drink too much, the next day is affected by it. Instead of awaking to a new day refreshed and alert, the mind and body remain dull and heavy. We are not free to relax and enjoy today because of the residue from yesterday. Yesterday is gone forever; it's no longer real or relevant but is merely a concept, a memory. To have our lives controlled and determined by the past is a denial of the present, and to deny the present is to deny reality itself.

As physical hangovers are inherited from the past so are psychological hangovers. How we were "brought up" plays a key role in determining our thoughts and feelings, and they are what direct our actions. Our actions are based on how we feel, our feelings are based on how we think, and our thoughts are based on information received from society, society being our parents, teachers, clergy, and various other experts and authorities. So we are not really our own person but are *their* person. We are formed in *their* image rather than in the image of truth or reality.

Now whether or not the suggestions we receive from others are true, right or useful is not the point; the point is that we have been effectively conditioned to see and hear from their perspective. But we are not them, we are us; we are unique. Our perspective is not better and not worse; it is only different. Consequently, there will be a discrepancy, a space between the way society says it is and the way we experience it. And in this space is where we experience our conflict and confusion, and where we lose our joy and spontaneity.

Becoming Spontaneously Conventional

As children, we are fully alive, free and innocent; we are full of wonder, curiosity and delight - but we are not civilized and not wise to the world. So in the interest of safety, culture and wisdom, it is necessary that we be "killed" a little bit, that certain "conditions" be placed on our behavior. We cannot be too free, for we must remember to "look both ways before crossing," share our possessions with others, say "Thank you," "You're welcome," "How are you?" "Have a nice day," etc. Thus we leave innocence and become conventional, standardized.

But this is not the final stage of our development; it is only the second of three stages. The first stage is being spontaneous but unconventional; the second is being conventional but unspontaneous. It is in one of these two stages where most of us spend our lives, and except for occasional glimpses now and then, never realize there is anything better or higher. The third stage is a combination of the first and second: *it's being conventional and spontaneous at the same time*. It's where what we do, think, and feel are simultaneous, where what comes out of us is a direct and immediate reflection of what is inside of us, and all of it in perfect accord with the situation we are in.

The third stage is achieved through emptying the mind of all past knowledge. It's to let go of all previously held positions as to the way life is, and to just be open-minded toward all experience, all the time. It's to assume the attitude of Descartes that "Perhaps everything we believe is false." It's to live every moment as if you were just born to it, as if nothing like this has ever happened before and never will again. It's to experience life without ever coming to a conclusion about it, for as soon as we do, the mind shuts and becomes unable to receive anything new. To conclude is to finish; but truth is infinite, it can never be finished; it just goes on unfolding, surprising and delighting for as long as we remain open to it and unexcited by it.

Reality Is A Reflection Of Our Beliefs

Reality faithfully follows our beliefs: If we believe we can be, do, or have something, we can; if we don't, we won't. It is in this way that belief controls and limits us. Therefore we must be careful about what we think, for as we are thinking we are also programming ourselves. Thinking is not the mind itself, but is the *tool* of the mind just as a computer keyboard is not the computer itself, but a tool that feeds or programs it. And just as you would not operate the keyboard indiscriminately, so you would not think or believe indiscriminately, for what you get out will be a mirror reflection of what you put in. A single negative thought, for instance, can ruin your whole day.

A person who holds to some belief or preconceived notion about the way life is, is the same as a computer with a "program." And just as a computer does not have a mind of its own except for its program, so a person with beliefs and positions does not have a mind of his own except for those beliefs and positions. His preconceptions *are* his mind, while his consciousness is totally absent. Incapable of original thought or experience, he then becomes a parrot where everything that comes from his mouth is either a verbatim transcript from some other source, or something he has rehearsed. If you say "this" he will say "that"; if you press "this" button he will react "this" way; if you press "that" button he will react "that" way. His life and mind are "set" so that he is no longer a human being but is now a mechanical being.

Preconceptions about life do not work because life is not conceptual, it is experiential. Life is not to be thought about - it is to be lived. You cannot taste an *image* of a strawberry; you must have the *actual* strawberry in order to be fulfilled. And no amount of believing or intellectualizing will ever give you the taste of it.

Belief Vs. Open-Mindedness

Instead of believing in a thing - be *open* to it. When you "believe" in something, you are, in effect, separating yourself from it; you are putting it on a pedestal, programming yourself to remain always apart from it. A belief is something that is always over the horizon somewhere and must always remain there. A belief is not an attainable thing but an ongoing exercise in fantasy like a carrot being held in front of our nose. Openness, on the other hand, allows you to taste and enjoy the carrot right here, now, and always. If you merely "believe" in truth, love, beauty, God, bliss, consciousness, abundance, then you will never experience such things. But if you are *open* to them - you will. To be open is to be empty, and whenever you are empty all that is good and positive in life rushes in to fill the void. If you would receive that which is higher, your mind must be in a state which is higher, and that is a state of openness or emptiness (which is the same as stillness).

To live in the mind and not reality is to live in a state of "limbo." Limbo means you are neither dead nor alive, but somewhere in between. You are alive in the sense that you know something exists, but are dead in the sense that you cannot experience it.

Being Emotional Vs. Being Creative

Thinking is an activity, and like desiring, it can either be emotional or creative. As a general rule of thumb, if thinking does not go somewhere in particular, does not solve some specific problem or achieve some conscious objective, then it is emotional. Believing, hoping, expecting, desiring, intellectualizing, daydreaming, fantasizing, resenting, complaining, worrying, and the like, can be identified as emotional because they are of a dead-end nature. They have no practical end. They just sap vitality and give nothing in return. Creative thought leads to and coincides with productive action. It brings problems and goals to resolution. There is no waste, no fat; each thought pulls its own weight and contributes coherently to some overall plan. In creative or recreational activity, you control the mind; in emotional activity, the mind controls you.

The question to ask is, who is in charge here, you or your mind? You are in control of your mind because you can *observe* it. The observer is always above the thing he observes. You can observe your thoughts and opinions; it is you who determines what is right, wrong, good, bad, valuable, useless, etc.; therefore, you can control or adjust these things to your convenience, conditioning, or habit. The point to grasp is that you *can* change your mind; you *do* have a choice. And the ultimate power of control always lies with the observer.

I say "ultimate" because, in a sense, thought controls us. The relationship between you and your mind is like that between you and your child: by merely observing him, you are controlling him but he is also controlling you because you *have* to be there; you are bound to observe him. Each controls the other, but you are the ultimate authority.

To Agree Is To Control

Notice that you don't have to *do* anything in order to control your mind or a situation. No mental activity is required. All that is necessary is the indifferent observation of it. The whole idea behind controlling a thing is the desire to bring it into agreement with your personal or biased perspective. You want things to fit in with your preconceived notions of how they should be. But if you're indifferent to what is happening, then you are in agreement with it already, so in effect, you already have control of it. *The situation is under control merely by virtue of your being in agreement with it.* By being in agreement with, or acceptant of a thought, feeling, situation, you "control" them so to speak. Nothing else has to be done. If, on the other hand, you are not observing in an indifferent manner, then you cannot be in agreement with it. Your view will then be different, separate, at variance from what is happening, so you will no longer be controlling the situation, it will be controlling you. If your child is having a temper tantrum and you are upset by it, then you have lost control. The child is now controlling you. But if, by remaining a lovingly detached observer, you do not get upset, the child will either stop crying if his discomfort is emotional, or if it's physical, you will then have the presence of mind to see and correct the problem. So the mind or situation is in control only when we are in agreement with it, and we are to the degree we're indifferent to it.

What is true of the mind is also true of the body and spirit: they are under control because we can observe them; we can see movement and feel feelings. And as long as we are in agreement with them, they are free to operate spontaneously. When the foot wants to move to a more comfortable position, it doesn't have to think about it, it just moves; when the spirit wants to feel sad, it just does so. And as the foot would not stay in an uncomfortable position unless we restricted it, so the spirit would not remain sad unless we restricted it. We restrict the spirit by disagreeing with it, by being averse to it, by viewing it prejudiciously instead of impartially.

Through disagreement, natural roles become reversed. What we would control, now controls us. What was subordinate, now dominates; the lesser dominates the higher; the child dominates the parent. What was a creative relationship with ourselves and the world now becomes an emotional one. As thoughts are the children of the mind, so movements are the children of the body, and feelings, that of the spirit. If the foot wants to move, let it move; if the spirit wants to cry, let it cry. When you agree with the sadness, when the sadness is all right with you, then there can be no more sadness. The spirit cries because you disagree with it - so simply stop disagreeing with it. Just let your children be. Don't interfere with them and they'll all be happy. Your body will be happy, your mind will be happy, and your spirit will be happy.

Attachment Vs. Detachment

When, because of disagreement, we cannot control our circumstances, the ego feels a great sense of insecurity. To the ego, being without control is synonymous with being without a self or without an identity. And without some identity how would it operate? How would it function? It would have no base from which to move, no foundation, no center. It would feel lost, strange, disconnected, unrelated.

Since we lost the true identity that was *within* us, the erroneous remedy will be to acquire a false identity from *outside* of us. We do this by egotistically identifying ourselves with particular groups, classes, cultures, beliefs, values, occupations, property, etc. We say, "I" am Irish, Italian, Hungarian, a Republican, a Democrat, a Hindu, a Jew, a Catholic, a father, a mother, a teacher, a doctor, a baker, etc. That is *who* I am, that is *what* Iam. I am not a nothing, I am these things - *and proud of it*!

There is nothing wrong, of course, with "birds of the same note" flocking together, nothing wrong with practicing or subscribing to a particular culture, religion or philosophy, or with taking positions on political and social issues, etc., but there is everything wrong with *emotionally* identifying with them. To emotionally identify with some belief or position means you have lost yourself to it; it means you have so equated yourself with it that it has replaced you as a free agent. You no longer exist, for where your true identity was, this belief now is. It is as if you have traded in your soul for it. And if someone should now hold a view different than yours, then he is the enemy because your belief is you, so an attack on it, becomes an attack on you personally. If someone steps on your flag, he is stepping on *you*; if someone scratches your car, he is scratching *you*.

The opposite of being identified with a thing is being detached from it. To be identified or attached is emotional; to be detached is creative. There is a fine line of difference between them: in detachment, you are just as totally committed to an ideal or project but instead of it being an "ego trip" it is a purely recreational or cultural one. Just as we are not our body, mind and spirit, but are above them, so we are not our race, religion, nationality, occupation, property, etc., but are above them as well.

All Things Are Equal In Their Differences

Everything in life, whether material, intellectual or emotional must eventually be transcended for whatever we do not rise above enslaves us and makes us miserable. Whatever we depend on for our happiness owns us in the sense that any pleasure we would receive from it is cancelled out by either the constant fear of losing it, or the constant anxiety for more and more of it.

We rise above our experience when we realize that, in the larger scheme of things, one possession, opinion, or feeling is no more or less valuable than any other - they are just different.

When we come to see that all things are the same on some level, we mature, we grow to a higher level. When growing up, we first identify with our little rural neighborhood where our view is very narrow. Everyone looks, thinks and acts the same way. We all go to the same church and read the same newspaper. We grow out of it and move to the city where life is more diverse. But even the city has to be transcended. Yes, there is variety but the differences are superficial: instead of one newspaper there are two, but the only difference is that one slants the news this way, the other, that way; instead of one church, there are two, but the only difference between them is that one interprets scripture this way, the other, that way. So we outgrow the city and become an international person, able to understand, appreciate, and relate to people of all races, customs, cultures and ideas. Here we finally see that there is essentially no difference between all the people and things of the world, that, *in their differences*, they are all exactly the same. My skin is just as black as yours is white; my nose is just as short as yours is long; my politics are just as conservative as yours are liberal, etc.

The world is like a glass windshield that has shattered into four billion interconnected pieces, each of which is a person. They are all of the same piece of glass; the only difference is that each reflects light at a slightly different angle. They are all of the same substance, but each expresses that substance according to his own unique perspective. There are no good pieces or bad pieces, no right pieces or wrong pieces, all there are, are *different* pieces.

With the understanding that, as far as reality is concerned, one person's opinion is no more or less valid than anyone else's, we outgrow the personal perspective and adopt a universal one. We realize that reality can't be seen with personal eyes but only with impersonal ones. So we want to empty the mind of all the attachments, identifications, characteristics and accumulations that constitute our persona and deal with life freely, directly, and open- mindedly.

The opposite of being a "personality" or "character" is being a medium or mirror. A mirror does not have any particular qualities or characteristics of its own, it simply reflects faithfully whatever it sees. The nature of a mirror is to be perfectly clear for the slightest blemish will affect the fidelity of its reflection. If it has any thoughts or beliefs of its own, then it will no longer be an honest mirror but a corrupt one which distorts everything it sees accordingly. If the mirror is to be effective, it cannot have a self of its own, it must be selfless; that is, it must have no notions of its own in order to be able to see and reflect with integrity.

We Have No Control Apart From Objective Reality

The idea that we are something apart from reality is an illusion. Our thinking gives us the false impression that we are in control. The more we "think" the more we imagine we are the masters of our lives. The fact is that apart from reality we are nothing; we have no *personal* control over our lives whatsoever. To the degree we are tuned with reality, life works for us; to the degree we are not, it doesn't. Our personal knowledge not only has nothing to do with it, but constitutes our being out of tune in the first place. This is the story of Adam and Eve who, as a result of "eating" knowledge lost their spontaneity and their connection to reality.

When the mind is still, empty, free of thought, you are then under the government of balance so are in tune with reality. Nothing else has to be done or thought about. The universe has already been thought out, all you have to do is flow along with it. But when you start thinking or following some belief system, then you have fallen under a false government and have left reality. Now you are worshipping idols instead of truth. Instead of letting what *is* govern your life, you are now letting your *beliefs* govern it.

Letting Go

Letting go of yourself will be both difficult and easy: difficult in the sense that, without all those positions and conditions you've wrapped yourself in, you would feel naked and vulnerable. But nakedness and vulnerability are the whole idea; they are the very essence of freedom. To be open and exposed means you have nothing to hide, nothing to defend, and therefore, nothing to fear or be anxious about. All fear is the fear that you are nothing, compounded by the fear that others will discover it. The fact is that you really are nothing and so is everyone else. So the first belief to let go of is the belief that your ordinariness is any more or less ordinary than anyone else's. You don't need to hide from the fact that you're equal to everyone else. If your gun misfires while trying to shoot someone, you don't need to apologize to him, he certainly isn't going to care. And in the same way, if you admit to another, through your openness, acceptance and sensitivity that you are equal to him, he certainly isn't going to care either.

Letting go will be easy in the sense that you don't have to add anything to yourself, but rather, to drop things you have accumulated. To hold on to something takes energy and effort, but to release a thing requires neither - you just drop it. Imagine that you are carrying all your knowledge in a shopping bag, years and years of accumulated information and misinformation are packed into it making it a very heavy load. To hold on to this bag day in and day out takes energy and effort, but to let it go all you have to do is relax your hand, release your grip and the bag falls by itself.

If information is so necessary to the conduct of your life, then how could you ever have enough of it? If you need information to live, then where would it stop? Where would it end? At what point would you consider your knowledge sufficient? If there is no end to it, then there can't be a beginning either; that is to say, if you are deficient in information right now, then you shall always be. The book that would provide you with the information you need to cope with this moment has not been written yet. And when it is, it will be immediately obsolete, for the situation that called for it will be gone and the new situation will have a completely different set of variables requiring yet another book that will also be obsolete on completion, and so on. In other words, by depending on knowledge gleaned from the past, you remain in the past yourself; you remain in a state of perpetual obsolescence. It's like being the trailer behind the car: the trailer not only wants to be exactly where the car is, but wants to be there at exactly the same time. The car is like reality, and the trailer is like the knowledge-dependent person who must always lag behind it. The information necessary to handle this moment intelligently must come from out of this moment, not from out of the past. It must come from within you, not from outside of you. Outside information is dead and gone; inside information (intuition) is alive and ever-present.

Knowledge from the past or from books is useful in only a general way, but reality is very specific. You can be prepared for a meeting generally but not specifically because there are too many variables involved. There is no way of knowing in advance the specific questions that will be brought up or which direction the discussion will turn and why. To be prepared to move in any direction with equal ease requires a mind that is open, empty, and still. A mind that contains anything at all will be restricted by those contents. Such a mind will not be able to "think on its feet" unless the questions that come up just happen to correspond with the predetermined answers it is carrying around. Which is unlikely, for reality does not conform to us, it is for us to conform to it. To have an answer without a question is just as useless as having a question without an answer. Open-mindedness means not having any answers or any questions either; it is to be totally empty so as not to impose limits on your own intelligence or common sense.

Think of that bag of positions you are carrying as being full of dead information like yesterday's newspaper, pages and pages of dead answers to questions life is never going to ask again, and each answer having the effect of limiting or diminishing you a little bit. Each premeditated answer uses up some of your intelligence in the same way that a computer's memory bank is used up, so that at any given moment you are operating at far below capacity.

As you let the newspaper go when finished, so let the moment go when it is finished. Enter each moment new, fresh, open, receptive. Keep your mind clear. Be ignorant like Socrates: Have no knowledge of your own but be impartially interested in the knowledge of others.

The law of reverse effort applies to "believing" as well as to any other activity. You are the opposite of what you think or believe: if you think you know it all, you know nothing; if you think you are wise, you are a fool; if you think you are educated, you are ignorant; if you believe you are great, you are common; if you believe you are the life of the party, you are a bore, and so on. "Believing," in and of itself, indicates just the opposite - that you are doubting. Belief and doubt are two sides of the same coin, so that it's impossible to have a belief about something without also having a doubt about it. To correct this imbalance, apply the "Double-Barreled Balancing Technique": depending on your personality, you can either *believe everything or doubt everything*: believe everything or believe nothing; doubt everything or doubt nothing. Those are the only two choices that reality offers and no split orders, substitutions or exceptions are allowed.

To let go, to surrender, to give up, all mean the same thing: to relinquish something lower so that something higher may operate; it means dropping the narrow, limited personality so that the higher potentiality within us may work in its place. The intelligent organism that we are is what we're surrendering to. When we give *up* or give *in*, the "up" or the "in" means our organism. When we go to sleep we trust it, we give up to it, so why can we not give up to it when awake as well?

Being A Receptacle

In order to experience the aliveness, consciousness, and joy of reality, we have to be receptive to it. Think of reality and yourself as two halves that join together inside of you. Reality or truth doesn't have a self or body of its own; it is a spirit like electricity and must live *through* us. Conversely, we do not have a spirit of our own but must live *from* it. We are merely receptacles into which this spirit may plug. Together we constitute reality; separate we exist as a falsity. Just as a toaster isn't "really" a toaster unless it's plugged into electricity, so we aren't "really" human unless plugged into the spirit.

And the way we become receptive to this spirit of truth is, again, to relax the mind to a complete standstill by keeping it free and clear of all content. When the mind is out of the picture we make direct contact with life; when it is not, life remains at arms length like a stranger, something we can never become intimate with, something we can never taste or touch. With an open mind we become fused to life. We become organically connected to it like the "head and tail of the same animal."

It is only through being so connected with life that we can know and respond intuitively and immediately. Intuition is not mysticism; it is common sense. It is operating with a clear conscience, a conscience that is unclouded and undisturbed by emotion. Intuition or common sense is being naturally smart, sharp, alert, insightful; it is the ability to notice a pattern in what's going on and to immediately pinpoint the significant aspect of it without having to *think* about it. When you see a work of art or design, for example, you know right off whether it "works" or not, whether you like it or not. You don't have to think about it; it's either compatible with your sense of harmony or it's not. Or if you were listening to a piano recital and a wrong note was struck, you would know it immediately, even without ever having heard the piece before or without ever having had any musical training. The music was flowing smoothly along when all of a sudden - an abrupt change, a note totally incompatible with the pattern or rhythm of what preceded and followed it. A sour note, and your whole body recoiled in instant recognition of it. This is intuitive knowing and it's an exact science to the degree you are sensitive and alert.

This is how it works: The organism that we are is whole and complete, and all its parts work together in a perfectly harmonious design. We, then, are harmony itself so certainly ought to recognize it when we see or hear it. If anything we see or hear is not harmonious, not "right," it will immediately disagree with us. What we are and what we perceive will not correspond. There will be a difference between what the organism knows is right and what we're seeing with our eyes. Thus we know instantly, directly, and without the intervention of thought the difference between the beautiful and the ugly, the good and the bad, the just and the unjust, the useful and useless, the true and the false, the right and the wrong. In other words, the value, morality, or truth of things are most accurately determined on a moment-to-moment, case- by-case basis, so never need to be formulated in advance. *Mis*-judging people and situations is caused by *pre*-judging them, for what's right in one case may be wrong in another. The only way to know the difference is to be still and open.

To be open is to be honest, and honesty is prerequisite to freedom. A false or artificial person can never be spontaneous and free, for he must be constantly on guard as to what he said or learned earlier. An artificial person must have a good memory but an honest person doesn't need one at all; an artificial person is defensive and secretive, always concealed and disguised, never himself. But an honest person is revealed, bare, exposed; he is what he is, simple, natural, ordinary, content; he is independent and self-sufficient; he stands on his own two feet, is his own psychologist and his own priest, his own expert and his own authority, his own teacher and his own hero. He has returned to the innocence of a child, only now, he is a man.

CHAPTER 6

CONTROLLING THE SITUATION

Power Over Influence is the Secret of Emancipation

How does one act in a way that is non-personal, non-emotional, non- egotistical? How do we act in accordance with our highest and best interests, and at the same time be impartial, selfless, and spontaneous? If we no longer have a "personal" self to identify with, then who are we and how do we behave? If we are just happy mediums, just creative, open-minded free spirits without thought, desire, or identity, how do we conduct ourselves in the world? How would our lives be structured? The answer is by:

Letting The Situation Determine Your Role And Letting The Role Determine Your Behavior

The "situation" is the relationship in which you find yourself at any given moment, your "role" is the particular part you play in that relationship, such as employer/employee, clerk/customer, husband/wife, parent/child, professional/client, etc., and the correct behavior for that part is governed by social custom or law.

Thus you act, but not according to your personal bias or ego; you act according to a role prescribed by the *situation*. Your ego has effectively been removed from the decision-making process; it has been stripped of all its discretionary powers. You now act according to *reality* rather than *person*ality. The situation is the highest worldly authority; it tells us who we are and how we shall respond, not the ego, not the mind. If a snake crosses your path, you don't *think* about stepping aside - you just step aside. Since the situation is the foundation upon which all our actions and responses are based, it follows that we deal with it as directly as possible. To the degree we do, we live naturally instead of mechanically. We move from moment-to-moment and role-to-role with the ease and grace of a ballerina rather than with the studiedness of an automaton. And the beauty of it is, we don't have to think about it; it's all unpremeditated, all unstressful. Freedom means not having to make any choices in life. All we have to do is know the situation we are in, know our role in it, and then *act* accordingly.

To Be Is To Be In Relationship

Since "acting" is our subject it will be useful to think in theatrical or literary terms. Let us consider, as Shakespeare has suggested, that "All the world's a stage and people, merely players." Think of yourself as being the main character in a play, and your moment-to-moment experience as being the different scenes in it. You, the protagonist, are the person around whom the play or story revolves. You are at the center of the action. Whatever is happening is happening with respect to *you*, not anybody else. In one scene you are at home with your family and playing the role of "husband" or "wife" or "Mother" or "Father"; in another, you are at work playing the part of a "co-worker" with respect to other co-workers, or the alternating roles of "manager" with your subordinates and "subordinate" with your managers. In other scenes, you are playing the role of a "spectator" at a performance, "participant" at a social gathering, "listener" with respect to music, "friend" with respect to a friend, and so on. These scenes are the ever- changing backgrounds, settings, and contexts in which you, the central character, operate.

Notice that in all these scenes, you are there in relation or connection to someone or something else. Even when you are alone, you are relating to yourself, to your aloneness, to the music you are listening to, etc. In a universe where all things are connected, it is impossible *not* to be related to something at any given moment. The key to right action is to be always aware of what that something is. If you don't know how your presence is immediately relevent or pertinent to a situation, you can't know what your proper role is either, and if you don't know what your proper role is, you will be either unresponsive, or your response will not be a true reflection of what is happening. It is essential, therefore, to consciously think of all situations, circumstances, and experiences in terms of being *relationships*.

To Be Real Is To Play A Role

Once reality is seen as being a relationship, it becomes obvious that the role you play in it is also "real." If reality is a relationship, and you play a role in that relationship, then it follows that the "role" you play is also "real" - not *absolutely* real, but real in the sense that it is *compatible* with reality. Roles are not you in the higher spiritual sense; they are you in the lower physical sense. In the spiritual sense your identity never changes; you are always the impartial observer who is above everything. On the physical level your identity must constantly change in order to accord with ever-changing conditions. Thus, by "playing a role" we *are* being "real"; we are being in tune with reality.

Put another way, your role is not *who you are*; it is *what you do*. It is your work, duty, function, position, or office. A "judge" is not *really* a judge but just *acts* as a judge when "on the bench." When he leaves the courthouse, he no longer acts as judge but as a "husband" with his wife, as a "father" with his children, as a "friend" with his friends, and so on. And likewise, "parents" are not *really* parents in the higher spiritual sense either, but just play the role of parents. That a role comes by way of a biological relationship rather than a social one does not make it any less a role. Reality does not differentiate between biology and society. All roles, regardless of their level or genesis, must be played in the orderly and principled manner that is appropriate to them. To the degree they are, there is harmony; to the degree they are not, there is conflict.

The conflict comes from confusing who we are with what we do. We are human *beings*, not human *doings*. "Being" is who we are; "doing" is just an act, just a part we play. Keeping the two in their place is just a matter of playing one's role consciously instead of unconsciously. The difference is merely one of attitude. Before, we did not think in terms of "playing a role." Not because we thought it was false, but because we were so egotistically identified with everything we did, that we believed we actually *were* all those parts we were playing. We could not separate the actor from the act. So the difference between conscious and unconscious role playing is that in the one case, you emotionally identify with your role, you think it is really you, and in the other case, you see yourself as being separate from it, as being above it. You see your role merely as a social formality, as a "hat" to be worn, not as something to be taken personally, but as something to be taken creatively.

The role itself is artificial, but you, the actor, are real. You are the artist, and your role is your medium. Playing a role does not mean you are not yourself; on the contrary, you are fully yourself, but *you are yourself within the context of your role*. A role provides the necessary vehicle or means by which you *can* express yourself authentically. To be authentic simply means to be uniquely yourself. And since you already are yourself, all that remains is to have some platform. Your family and social roles provide that platform. If you are playing the role of a waiter, businessperson, housekeeper, artist, doctor, clerk, parent, it is your own unique spirit that distinguishes you from all others playing the exact same role. Your role, like the body in which you live, is superficial, but the spirit that animates it and gives it expression is authentic.

The Real Actor Can Play Any Role

The mark of an authentic actor is his adaptability. He can move with equal ease into any role, while the emotional, artificial actor is limited in the types of roles he can play. The artificial actor is like a painter who can paint landscapes but not seascapes, or like a novelist who can write mystery novels but not romance novels, or like a salesperson who can sell oranges but not apples. These are not true artists. A true painter can paint anything, a true writer can write anything, a true salesperson can sell anything.

The authentic actor has the flexibility of a chameleon. A chameleon's color is not fixed, but changes in accordance with his environment: when on a brown tree, he turns brown; when on yellow leaf, he becomes yellow; when on a green leaf, green. If you asked him what color he was, he could only say, "It depends on the situation," or, if he was a saleschameleon, he might say, "What color do you want?" Similarly, when the authentic actor is in Rome, he dances the tarantella; when in Tel Aviv, he sings Havah Nagilah. If he's poor, he does without; if rich, he lives lavishly. When at a wedding banquet, he plays the role of "celebrant"; at a funeral, he becomes a "mourner." If the chameleon did not change colors he would stand out. Likewise, if a person was cheerful at a funeral and somber at a wedding, he too would stand out. He would not be in harmony with the situation, not be connected to it.

We say such a person doesn't know how to act. He doesn't know his part. He is isolated from the situation rather than related to it. This isolation makes him a stranger instead of a participant.

He may not like the situation he's in, but that's beside the point. The point is, he's there, so he's obliged to act accordingly. Liking or disliking are emotional considerations; they are irrelevant to the reality of the situation and one's role in it. Reality is not concerned with what we like or dislike; it's only concerned with what *is*, and that our response is *equal* to it.

The authentic actor doesn't have a "self" with which to like or dislike. He has no passions, feelings, or desires of his own. Whatever he feels is not for himself, but accords with the situation he's in or the person he's with: if you are hurt, he is hurt; if you are happy he is happy. Whatever you want is what he wants; wherever you want to go is where he wants to go. His whole being is determined by you. Of himself he is already fulfilled, already "there," so he's incapable of doing anything else but giving. This is called love, and it has nothing to do with personality or emotionality; it has to do with being sensitive to the person or situation, and letting him or it determine who you will be and how you will respond.

Keeping A Respectable Distance

All relationships in the play of life consist of two corresponding parts, each of which has a specific identity in terms of how it is expected to behave toward the other. "Correctness" in behavior does not proceed arbitrarily, but in a systematic or methodical manner. Everything in the universe works in accordance with law and order, and correct behavior is no exception to the rule. In order for society to function in an orderly and efficient way, it's necessary that its members act in conformance with certain conventions of behavior. The clerk is expected to behave in a certain way with respect to his customer, and the customer is expected to behave in a certain way with respect to the clerk. And likewise in the relationships between professional and client, teacher and student, parent and offspring, husband and wife, employer and employee, etc. Each has a social obligation and responsibility to act towards the other in a manner that's in character with the role being played.

Convention is not only social law, it's universal law as well, which is to say, that to the degree you follow convention, your actions will be successful, and to the degree you do not, they will not be successful.

The universal law that governs all social intercourse is the "love/wisdom principle" of not influencing or interfering with the proper role of another, and not allowing another to influence or interfere with your proper role. "Correctness" in behavior, then, means *keeping a respectable distance* from your counterpart in a given relationship so as not to violate the integrity of that relationship.

Being Firm And Considerate

Maintaining this integrity will require both *firmness* and *considerateness*. To not permit a person's office, sex, money, or position to influence or intimidate you will require unflinching firmness of character. To likewise not influence others will require a sensitive considerateness. "Keeping your distance" is *what* you have to do; being firm and considerate is *how* you do it.

Firmness is being direct and unambiguous. It is saying what you mean and meaning what you say. When you are playing your roles appropriately, you are free to be confident, free to speak plainly and simply. It is the person who doesn't know who he is, who doesn't know he is merely playing a role who halters, falters, and flinches, who is irresolute and indefinite, who is easily suggestible, tempted, moved, and pressured.

When you are playing your roles with integrity, you do not have to get along with others - they have to get along with you. It is *you* who are real; therefore, it is *you* to whom others must answer, *you* to whom others must become equal. In any situation it is the person playing his role most appropriately and selflessly who sets the standard for the others.

Considerateness balances firmness. Being considerate is regarding and appreciating others. An essential human need is to be appreciated for what we are. We are all special in the sense that there is no one in the world quite like us. While being different is nothing to be proud of, it is, however, something to be recognized. Appreciating others is a form of love and wisdom which means we don't practice it because it is nice or because we may derive some benefit from it, we practice it because it is compatible with reality, so we really have no choice in the matter. People *are* different; relating to them, therefore, implies relating to their differentness. If we are to relate to a person at all, we must recognize and appreciate him; there is no other way. To be with a person and not appreciate him is to not *really* be with him; it is to be with him on the most superficial and meaningless level, a level from which only boredom could come. Appreciating and recognizing the specialness of others *is* nice and we certainly *will* benefit from it, but that's not why we do it; we do it because it's essential to authentic relationship and so to the fulfillment of being.

We appreciate a person by simply being aware of him, by being sensitive to him. Awareness and sensitivity require energy, and merely applying energy to a person, in and of itself, is to appreciate him. It is to listen to a person with undivided attention. Your mind cannot be divided between listening and being somewhere else, or listening and casting judgment. *You are listening for the purpose of understanding* - nothing else. To understand a person means you are relating, you are communicating. Communication is the experience of being understood, and to be understood is to be recognized and appreciated.

To Know You Is To Know Me

With understanding comes tolerance and patience. How can you be intolerant or impatient with someone you understand? You can't be, for to understand a person is to realize that he is essentially just like you. Only the ignorant are intolerant; they "think" everyone is separate from them. They do not see the connection; they do not see that we are all in the same boat, heading in the same direction, and totally dependent on each other for getting there. I cannot get there without you, nor you without me. By appreciating and understanding each other we learn the things we both have to learn in order to get where we both are going. We are all on different paths and levels, consciously or unconsciously seeking for the missing pieces to our respective puzzles. You hold the key to the pieces I am missing, and I hold the key to those you are missing. When we cross paths, regardless of the context or the pretext, it is for the purpose of discovering something about ourselves, something necessary to our evolution. Relationship with people and things is the only means by which to see who we really are, and how we may more efficiently get to where we are going. So by appreciating others we are really appreciating ourselves; by understanding others we are really understanding ourselves; by finding others we are really finding ourselves.

Patience and tolerance are understanding that everyone is "perfect" as he is right now, "perfect" in the sense that whatever level a person happens to be operating on is the level that is right for him at that particular time. Where he's at with respect to his growth is exactly where he's supposed to be at with respect to his growth. It is impossible for a person to be different than what he is at any given moment. In that sense, he is perfect, he is genuine. If a person is stupid,unconscious, or ignorant, he is genuine in his stupidness, unconsciousness, or ignorance. And even if he is artificially those qualities, that is, even if he is acting stupid for whatever reason, he is still genuine-genuine in his falseness. However a person behaves is perfectly equal to him, it is in perfect accordance with his present state of mind. As far as he is concerned, he is right, so in the eyes of reality he is also right. The correct response, then, the response most compatible with this reality - is to excuse him, to forgive him, to overlook his offense, to make allowance for him, to agree with him.

Agreeing with a person's view doesn't mean you claim to hold the same view; it means you *understand* it, you appreciate the *reason* behind his arriving at that particular view. In that sense, you are in agreement. He is indeed right, right according to *his* reasoning.

If a person holds certain religious or political views, for instance, or ideas on the best way to invest one's money, improve one's health, control the traffic on Main Street, etc., it is for you the interested, impartial listener to "agree" with those views by understanding them. Being agreeable simply means to always stand on the side of the fence your counterpart happens to be standing; it is to "stand in his moccasins" and view the world through his unique perspective. If his reasoning does happen to be faulty, the process of appreciating or understanding his view usually results in his discovering the error for himself.

This, discovering-the-error-for-oneself is the principle behind psychological healing. To "see more clearly" and to be "healed" are one and the same thing. "Healing" is another word for problem solving. In the process of understanding a person we use the same method as in creative problem solving: we convert a person's general statements into more and more specific ones. We keep feeding his general statement or question back to him by asking what, where, when, why, or how, until we get to the bottom of it. If someone says he's voting for a certain political party and you ask why, etc., in the process of his becoming more specific for *your* understanding, it also becomes clearer to *him*, because your questioning requires him to see the issue from a different (unbiased) angle.

Good conversation is both a "technique" and is "natural" at the same time. Being natural is a technique in the sense that you are conducting yourself in an orderly way. You are not really *doing* anything; you are just *being* something; you are being yourself within the context of your role. Just being yourself has a therapeutic affect on others; you don't have to do anything. When you are calm, those around you become calm automatically. But when you are not yourself, you are nervous, and cause those around you to become nervous. The relaxed person is nourishing, we tend to gravitate in his direction; the nervous person has a toxic affect on us, we tend to avoid him. The nervous person is unable to appreciate or understand another for he is too self-centered, too self-conscious, too into himself. Consequently, there can be no communication between him and others, no growth, no healing, no uplifting or fulfilling of the spirit. He loses and his counterpart also loses. But all is not lost for the empty experience teaches him something that can be used in the future, so that eventually, he overcomes his selfishness and becomes his real and relaxed self again.

Distinguishing The Role From The Person

Personal feelings have nothing to do with a right relationship, for taking one's role in a personal way is the very thing that corrupts, breaks down, disorders the relationship. This means that when you are working as a police officer, for instance, you do not get angry at the law breaker. Anger indicates you are regarding the matter personally rather than officially. That a person chooses to speed or pass a red light has nothing to do with you as a person; it has to do with you as an official. Your becoming angry is to confuse your role with your personality which is to violate reality or the law of balance. The law says your role and your person must be kept separate. You are not your role but merely the actor. The secret of relaxation lies in the understanding of this distinction. To become emotional while in an "official" relationship is to contaminate that relationship. It is, of course, difficult to be personally unmoved while witnessing a person driving in a way that endangers innocent lives, but your feelings are none of your business. Your business is to act according to statute or to the standards of your profession. This is what distinguishes the cultivated from the ignorant, the professional from the amateur, the emotional from the creative.

Not Violating The Integrity Of The Relationship

All roles are professional in the sense that they are played, not according to personal feelings, but according to the dictates of the role itself. And since there is *never* a time when we are not playing some role, there is *never* a time when we act according to personal feelings.

Keeping a respectable distance between one anothers' role means we respect the sanctity of the individual; we respect the inviolable privacy of the individual. We don't get too familiar with anyone and don't allow anyone to get too familiar with us. "Familiarity breeds contempt" because it is an invasion of privacy. To have our privacy invaded is to have our very soul or center taken over so that we are no longer ourselves but are now laid open to exploitation. The key to being exploited, manipulated, or dominated is to let someone (or something) get personal with you. The more personal he gets, the more he controls you. As he "invades" your person, your soul becomes displaced by his soul, so to speak; his will subliminally replaces your will.

Friendship is only appropriate between friends, not between seller and buyer, professional and client, employer and employee, etc. And even between friends, or rather, especially between them, we never get too familiar but respect each others' individuality.

The same principle applies within the family, we regard each others' privacy through behaving in strict conformance to role. The father and mother guide and nurture, and the children listen and obey. The family, as in any successful organization or government, works according to a hierarchy of one leader, one second, one third, etc. The father acts as the head, the mother acts as the second, the eldest child, as the third, and so on. Any reversal of roles, such as the children controlling the parents or the mother acting as the head instead of the father, will cause a breakdown in the family, as it would in any organization. The sergeant has to obey the captain, the worker has to obey the manager, the vice-president has to obey the president, and so on; otherwise the thing can't work.

Of course, the head of the household must act in a manner appropriate to that position. He cannot use that "official" position for his own personal gratification, but only for the good of the family as a whole. With position comes responsibility The French term *noblesse oblige* means the "head" has an obligation and responsibility to act in a way that befits such a position. It is for your wife and children to respect your role, but it's for you to be unfailingly worthy of that respect.

Our proper role with respect to our children is one of steward or manager. Children are not our personal property in the sense that we own them and can do with them as we will. A child is an individual in his own right and that is how he must always be respected. We as parents serve merely as the physical mediums through which he can be born, and as his physical caretakers until he comes of age. It's not for us to affect his individuality in any way, but only to nourish and nurture it. As a property manager doesn't make renovations without permission from the owner, so we don't renovate or change the child without his permission. In the first place, a child is too young to give us permission, and in the second place, he has no need to be changed. High intelligence and happiness are inherent in every child. All we have to do is cultivate that potential by just letting him be himself by way of sensitivity and patience.

We want to treat him as if he already were his full potential. The child becomes the way he is treated. If we treat him childishly, he stays a child; he remains always short of his possibilities instead of always equal to them. But on the other hand, if with respect to his age, he is regarded as an independent and responsible individual, he naturally rises to the occasion.

Finally, what is our role with respect to ourselves; that is to say, with respect to the whole of existence, and what behavior is appropriate to that role? Our role, in personal terms, is that of a son or daughter, and our expected behavior is to listen and obey. Our relationship to our spiritual "parents" is exactly the same as that to our physical parents. We are the offspring of a powerful, intelligent, and loving organism. This organism infinitely nourishes and guides us, but only to the degree we obey or listen to its law of balance. And the way we obey this law is by allowing the situation we are in to determine what our role will be, and then simply playing that role firmly, correctly, and impersonally.

PART THREE

THE PRACTICE OF BEING MENTALLY AWARE

CHAPTER 7

OBJECTIVE AWARENESS

Perfect Objectivity Illuminates the Subtleties of Existance

Objectivity is a *detached awareness* of whatever we see, hear, think, feel, and do. As the last chapter spoke of being personally disconnected from the roles we play, this chapter will speak of being personally disconnected from the body, mind and spirit. As we are not the roles we play, we are also not the thoughts we think, the feelings we feel, the body we move, or the eyes and ears that see and hear, but are the indifferent witness who is above them all.

To be aware is to be mindful or heedful of something, and to be detached is to "step back" in order to experience that something just as it is, meaning, without personal or emotional involvement. In other words, being detached is:

Seeing With The Eyes Instead Of The Mind

It is seeing a thing without commenting on how beautiful or ugly it is, without criticizing or judging as to how right or wrong it is, without complaining or grumbling about it, and without desiring that it be in any way different than it actually is. We want to experience life as a fact, not as a figment of the imagination; we want to experience life in its innocence and nakedness, not clothed in the projections of our fantasies and expectations.

In order to experience life we cannot think about it. Thinking is the killer of life; thinking precludes life, it steps in place of it. Where *life* would be, *thinking* is. If something is beautiful or ugly, then that is what it is; there's no need to intellectualize it or comment on it. Just see the fact of it and let it go. If you want to ask questions about it, if you want to ask why and wherefore, then you have begun moving away from truth. There is, of course, nothing wrong with intellectual inquiry, that is, as long as you are aware that you're talking *about* truth and not *to* it, as long as you are aware that all discussion and commentary are merely recreational, social, or academic. Questions and answers about a thing are always subordinate to the thing itself, they are always secondary, peripheral activities. Discussing them only leads in circles because the truth has already come and gone, never to return. The point has already past so all commentary becomes moot. You see a beautiful sunset and your spirit is moved - that is the beginning and the end of it. To ask why is to leave reality and enter into mental activity which is a step downwards. You have already had it all, so anything further will be going backward. The libraries are filled with thousands of books explaining why the sunset is beautiful, and even if you could study them all, it would still not equal the knowledge contained in a single objective glance at a real sunset.

To experience life really and truly is to experience it joyfully. There is no difference between truth and joy. The closer you come to truth the closer you come to joy; the further from truth, the further from joy. Truth and joy are the absence of emotion; fantasy and suffering are the presence of it.

Detachment Is The Key To Increased Awareness

Awareness is the proof and measure of our aliveness. Being aware or conscious is the only means we have of confirming the existance of life. The more conscious we are of what is happening around us, the more alive we are; the less conscious, the less alive. Awareness, then, is the very essential, very central thing; it is the thing whose quality we want to improve. The higher the quality of our awareness, the higher the quality of our lives. The more sensitive, perceptive, alert we are, the more we penetrate into life and experience the infinite beauty of it. And the natural means by which we increase our level of awareness is through material, intellectual, and emotional detachment. The more detached we are, the more aware; the more aware, the more happily alive, intelligently responsive, and creatively powerful.

Acknowledging Your Biasedness

The basic attitude of reality is to assume and accept the fact that we are indeed personally biased with respect to practically all that we experience. It is not a question of maybe we are or to what degree we are - but that we are - period. Being present in the flesh, in and of itself, implies the existance of a bias. The point to grasp is that we do not *have* a bias, we *are* a bias.

Overcoming this original handicap, sin, or disease is to first assume and accept that you have it, and then to rise above it, to neutralize it, to live in such a way as to be unaffected by it: Just as we spontaneously remember to always stay within a few hours of a source of food so as not to starve, so we must spontaneously remember to always stay detached in our outlook so as not to fall into falsity or error.

To this end, it will be useful to think of yourself as being like a company or corporate organization with the mind, body, and spirit serving as your three key employees. The mind is your manager who does the planning and organizing for you, he is your brains or your computer; the body acts as your eyes and ears and also does all the legwork for you; and the spirit informs you as to whether or not everything is operating effectively and efficiently. The spirit is your accounttant or the conscience of the company. If you are not enjoying a "profit" because your plan, concept, or outlook is not right, or because your activities are not organized or being carried out properly, the spirit lets you feel it so you can stop to make the necessary course corrections. Thus your proper relationship is one of employer/employees, and your goal is to function as a single unit.

In order for an organization to operate successfully, the employer must control its employees and not vice versa; that is, we control the mind, body, and emotions; they don't control us. The way the employer maintains control, as we have seen, is by keeping a proper distance from his employees so that their respective roles don't conflict. We allow them to play their roles without our influencing or affecting their report, and we likewise, don't allow their report to personally influence or affect us. In this way, the parts work together for the good of the whole.

They are independent of each other and in harmony at the exact same time.

Detachment Is The Key To Self-Control

Controlling the mind and being detachedly aware of its activity are one and the same thing. By observing thoughts from a distance we control those thoughts - that's all there is to it; nothing further has to be done. Detached awareness, in and of itself, is the controlling factor. We are not interested in stopping or changing thought activity, but just in observing it as it is. By observing it as it is, we control it. Mental activity is like a child at play: to control him, we don't have to bridle him, just watch him. By watching him we control him. He can't begin to get into mischief because we're right there, we're right on top of the situation. The same with the mind: negative or misleading thoughts cannot begin to fester and harm us because we're right there at the very moment of their inception. By observing thoughts in a detached way, it becomes obvious that they can have no control over our feelings and actions unless we permit them to. We needn't feel bad about negative thoughts nor excited about positive ones. It is our nature to be well regardless of thought activity. To not be well indicates we are not ourselves, not in control; it indicates instead, that our mind or emotions are in control.

Socrates condensed all wisdom into two words - "Know thyself." And the way to know yourself is to detachedly observe yourself, to detachedly observe your mind. By watching your mind from a distance, you learn first hand who you are and why you act as you do. To the degree possible, notice all mental activity or stimulation; just pay attention to it as it is wherever and whenever it occurs. When you are thinking about going out to a restaurant, *know* that's what you're thinking about; when you are playing tennis and thinking you might win or lose notice yourself thinking those thoughts; if you're reflecting on a problem at work, watch yourself thinking the matter over and deciding on a course of action; when you find yourself daydreaming or musing, catch yourself doing it. Are you thinking of what you will wear, what you will say, what might be the response to what you say? Thinking of hurting someone, helping someone? Thinking of money, food, sex, reading, writing, retirement? Be aware that you are. And even when there is no thought activity at all, be conscious of that too. By persistently and choicelessly observing your thoughts in this way, you will soon break the false identity or attachment you have with them and so regain control in the process. Once you know you can control your thoughts, it will occur to you that you can control your whole life!

Your attitude with respect to all thoughts is that they are all alike; they are all the same to you. One thought is just as good or bad or right or wrong as any other. We don't feel guilty about the one, nor saintly about the other. From the perspective of a detached, impartial observer, there's no difference between a negative thought and a positive thought. They're both just thought, period. In other words, "No matter how you slice it, it's still baloney."

The rule of thumb is this: if it exists in the mind, no matter how lowly or how noble, it is not real but a concept or an illusion. It may or may not become real later, but at this stage, it's just imagination. And it's just this detachment that'll give you the power to wisely discriminate between which thoughts you'll discard, and which you'll proceed to convert into reality.

Increasing Emotional Awareness

We control emotions the same way we control thought, by observing them from a distance. By witnessing our feelings without attachment, we effectively correct the wrong relationship we've been having with them. We put emotion back in its proper place - as the employee not the employer, as the subordinate not the superior. Feelings are to inform not to control. When a feeling arises for or against something, whether negative, positive, painful or pleasurable, do not react to it in any way, but just watch it with calm disinterest.

If someone is behaving inappropriately, and you become irritated, just observe the fact of your irritation and nothing else. We are not concerned with whether the irritation is right or wrong; we are only concerned with the fact that it *exists*. If irritation is who or what you are in that moment, then be aware of it, be fully cognizant of it. Admit, accept, acknowledge that you are irritated.

If you can stand back and see your agitation clearly, it cannot fail to occur to you that this irritation was not caused by the other person; it originated with *you*; it is of *your* doing, *your* responsibility. Someone else didn't do it to you; you did it to yourself; you allowed it. Your feelings have taken you over and an outside agency is pulling the strings or pressing the buttons. Instead of observing that person's behavior from a distance, you got emotionally involved. You violated the integrity of whatever role you happened to be playing at the time. You took a social or family situation and made it personal. If a person acts improperly, it's not your personal concern; it's the concern of your role, so it's for you to respond according to that role. If you were a judge and were provoked by a lawyer, you would hold him in "contempt." The "contempt" the judge "feels" is not personal but official. In the same way, if your son or daughter were acting "out of order," the matter would be handled parentally not personally. And likewise in the case of friends or strangers, the offended party would not react personally but in a manner appropriate to a friend or to a stranger in accordance with the situation.

As with thoughts, we want to observe pleasant and unpleasant feelings as if they were of equal value, not merely as a device to increase awareness; but because, as far as reality is concerned, they *are* equal. Reality is not concerned with whether you are feeling sad or happy, bored or interested, guilty or blameless, doubtful or confident, angry or tolerant, etc. As far as reality is concerned, they're all just the same; they're all *just* feelings. Reality is like a cup - totally indifferent to what's poured into it. It doesn't accept one beverage over another but is equally receptive to and unaffected by *whatever* is poured into it. Similarly, a flashlight doesn't shine differently on some things than others; it shines equally on everything. And a flashlight doesn't change according to what it shines on either; both the beautiful and the ugly have no affect on it; it remains itself, just an impartial, detached flashlight.

If we can remain in reality by adopting the attitude of the cup or the flashlight, all fear and conflict would be eliminated. Fear is always of the unknown, and conflict is always of one feeling or thought against its opposite. If you know that *life consists of nothing but negative and positive thoughts and feelings*, then you know everything; you know all there is to know. And if you know that *the negative and the positive are exactly alike*, then there can be no conflict. You know all there is to know, and you know how to respond to it - there's nothing else! Now you are free; now you are truly sophisticated, educated, cultivated. You know universal convention and can move within it with freedom, ease, and confidence. Now you can relax and enjoy.

Whatever comes into your cup, whether pleasant or unpleasant, embrace it without discrimination. Do not wrestle with it, argue with it, or entertain it in any way; do not love it, hate it, or fear it; do not accept it and do not reject it, but just be indifferently aware of it. You are playing the role of a cup and the appropriate behavior for a cup is to not get attached to the contents but to keep an emotional distance from them. Do not allow your contents to push, pull, or tempt you but remain firmly in the center of them. Do not indulge them and do not repress them, but just observe them from a distance. When you break the identification with your contents, you're no longer subject to them; you then no longer react robotically but in spontaneous accordance to what you know is right in each moment.

Increasing Sensual Awareness

The five sense organs fall under the "body" or "physical" category. The idea here is to keep a little space between the sense organs and the objects they sense. It's to sense things independent of your thoughts or feelings about them; it's to be keenly alert and responsive to what you perceive, yet personally removed.

Be more indifferent to odors. Is the smell gross like the secretion ejected from a skunk, or is it pleasant and appealing like the aroma of fresh-baked bread? Is it pungent and pervasive like garlic or Limburger cheese, or is it sweet and delicate like the perfume of a flower or the bouquet of a good wine? Let the *nose* discriminate between odors, but let the emotions regard all odors as being the same, as being *just* odors.

Be more indifferent to internal and external physical feelings. Is a thing warm or cold, moist or dry, soft or hard? Is it smooth like satin, or gritty and grainy like sandpaper? Notice any physical pain, tension, or discomfort. Where exactly is it, and what is the quality or character of it? Is it in the shoulders, stomach, lower back or in the head? What part of the head, front, back, or side? How far forward or back? How small or large an area does it take up? Is it a dull pain, or is it a sharp, piercing, biting or throbbing pain? The mental energy you direct toward pain, whether physical or emotional, is the same energy that relaxes that pain. To pay extremely close attention to your discomfort is all that's necessary to controlling or reversing it. According to the law of "mind over matter," it's impossible for pain and awareness to exist in the same spot at the same time. The only problem, of course, is that we're not aware, not objectively aware.

Be more indifferent to how a thing tastes. Is it sweet like honey and strawberries, or sour, tart and tangy like lemon or vinegar? Is it salty like ham and pork, or bland like bean curd? Is it bitter, briny, minty, metallic, rancid, nutty, peppery, acrid, spicy, zesty? Let the flavors begin in your mouth and end in your mouth. Don't let them travel to the emotions to be distorted. Let the *tongue* discriminate between tastes, but let the emotions regard all tastes as being equal.

The key to increased awareness is for each organ or faculty to know its proper place: it's for the tongue to taste the thing, emotions to report on the harmony or savoriness of the thing, and the mind to communicate or express it. Before you can express what you sense, you first have to be impressed by it.

Be more indifferent to sound. What do you hear, and what is the quality and character of that sound? Is it a clang, a bellow, a blare, a rattle, rustle, screech, chatter, crash, hiss, hum, murmur, pop, splash, squeak, sputter, fizzle, swish, tinkle? Is it loud and piercing like a siren, or soft and gentle like the purring of a kitten? Is it clear and distinct, or muted, faint, subdued, distant? Is it resonant or dissonant, full or hollow, boisterous or mellow? Is the rhythm monotonous like a whine or melodious like a song? Is it a high frequency sound like that of a flute or a whistle, or a low frequency one like that of a tuba? Is it harsh and jarring like a fingernail scraping against a chalkboard, or is it soothing and harmonious like a strain from a Brahm's lullaby? Let sounds originate in your ear and end in your ear. Do not allow them to travel to the mind or to the emotions to be contaminated. Let the ear discriminate between sounds, but let the emotions regard all sound as being just the same, as being *just* sound.

Be more indifferent to what you see. Look at people without comment or judgment; look at their sizes, shapes, postures, movements, gestures, and facial expressions. Notice how light or dark things are, how transparent or opaque, pale or vivid, symmetrical or asymmetrical. Look at how blue the sky is, how low or high the clouds hang. Look at how tall, craggy, and colorful the mountains are, how deep the valleys are, how wide the canyons are. Look at the shape and greenness of the leaves on a tree, and the texture and brownness of the bark. Notice how thick the fog and haze are, how tumultuous a storm is, and how the raindrops splash on the pavement. See how placid the lake, how tremendous the ocean, how swift and powerful the river, how clear and bubbly the brook, how delicate the mist on a flower.

When the senses are detached from the intellect and the emotions, things are perceived more clearly and vividly. It's like a veil or filter has been removed and you are seeing life as if for the first time. Before, everything was taken for granted, now, all things become interesting and significant. All things are seen to have a life, personality, and consciousness of their own. They are all communicating with each other on some level - and communicating with us as well. The language is subtle; to hear it will require a mind that is open, receptive, detached, and still. Reality is as shy as a bird and the slightest movement will frighten her away. But through perfect unobtrusiveness, she will feel related to you. She will light on your shoulder and she will reveal herself to you.

Increasing Physical Awareness

Breaking the attachment with the *body* is likewise achieved by viewing it from a distance. You want to observe the body's parts, shapes, postures, actions and reactions as if they didn't belong to you. To the degree possible, regard the body as if you were standing outside of it instead of inside of it. This will give the proper perspective.

As you go about your business, try to catch yourself in the *middle* of some position or activity. By this I mean, to notice what you are doing without giving yourself any warning, as if you were taking a candid photograph of yourself. For example, as you are reading these words, quickly glance over at your right hand and regard it as though it belonged to someone else. Just stop and look at it for a minute without moving it and without your mind entering into it. Notice the position of the thumb and fingers; notice the color of the skin, its texture, lines, and pores. Look at the knuckles, veins, hair, and nails. Do the same thing when you find yourself lying down, sitting, standing, walking, etc., sneak up on yourself, so to speak, and notice your posture or position as if apart from it.

Finding, discovering, knowing yourself simply means *remembering* yourself, remembering that you are indeed above, separate, and in control of yourself. And once you regain dominion over yourself, you simultaneously regain dominion over the world as well, for the two are not separate. Harmony within translates to harmony without. As you make sense, so does the world; as you fall into order, so does the world; as you become beautiful, so does the world. Detached awareness is simply the means by which to both trigger or stimulate this recollection, and to maintain it as well.

The theory behind this strategy of detachment is that in order to become natural, we must first become aware of our *un*naturalness; before we can know the truth of ourselves, we must first become aware of our falseness; before we can know pleasure, we must first go through the pain; and in the same way, in order to become spontaneously *un*self-conscious, we must first be deliberately *self*-conscious. It is necessary to pass through the night in order to reach the day, to pass through the negative in order to reach the positive. The negative is the bridge to freedom. We begin with the negative because that is the condition we happen to be in, that is the condition we, through inheritance, happen to be born in.

In all activity, be conscious of *what* you are doing and *how* you are doing it. Again, these are the only two questions awareness is concerned with. Awareness is not concerned with *why* you are doing a particular thing, that question should've been asked *before* you started doing it. Now that you are doing it, the only relevant questions are "what" and "how."

"Why" is an intellectual question, but life is not intellectual; it is experiential. Life is not to be thought about and questioned. Thinking and questioning are academic and miss the whole point. Life is to be known directly, immediately, wholly, and completely. Remember, we want to live in such a way as to be independent of the mind and the emotions. We want to experience life in and of itself, without their influence and interference. And the way we accomplish this is by being detachedly attentive to *what* we are doing and *how* we are doing it. Nothing else.

What kind of work do you do and how do you do it? If you are a manager, what are you managing and how are you managing it? If you are a trial attorney, what is the evidence you are presenting and how are you presenting it? If you are a surgeon, what procedure are you performing and how are you performing it? If you are working on an assembly line, what are you assembling and how are you assembling it?

When smoking cigarettes, notice how you hold the cigarette and how you flick the ashes. Notice the smoke being inhaled and exhaled. How does it smell? How does it taste and feel in your mouth and on your throat? The eating experience uses all of the five senses. Be aware of the sizzle, the smells, the colors, tastes and textures. Sexual activity also uses all of the senses. Be aware of how your partner looks, feels, smells, sounds and tastes. In conversation, what are you saying and how are you saying it? What exercises do you do and how? What leisure activities are you involved in and how are you involved?

In listening to music or viewing a work of art, notice how compatible it is with your highest sense of harmony, and notice what feelings they evoke. When reading or watching a drama, be aware of what the main character wants, what's preventing him from getting it, how he goes about achieving it, how he succeeds or fails and what is the theme or moral of the story. Be conscious that your own life has these same dramatic elements. What do you want? What is hindering you? How are you going about attaining it? What obstacles are you struggling to overcome? What lessons must you learn? And what is the theme and meaning of your own life?

By experiencing life in this impartial and detached way, you come out of your self and evolve to the third and final stage of growth. The first stage, again, is that of the free and innocent but unconventional youngster; the second stage is that of the conventional person, but one who has lost his freedom, innocence, and naturalness in the process; the third stage is that of the conventional, socially adept person, but one who has *regained* his freedom, innocence, and naturalness.

CHAPTER 8

CONTROLLING THE MIND

Practice is the Orderly Implement for Securing Excellence

Meditation practice is the most powerful tool for achieving and maintaining objectivity. We are unconsciously operating on a slant and need a little push to get back into balance. Meditation provides that necessary push. Becoming objective on your own is like trying to push a stalled car by hand, it's extremely difficult to move from a dead stop, but once you get it rolling a bit it's easy to keep rolling. In returning to balance, we likewise have this inertia to overcome in the beginning, and meditation is the natural technique by which to overcome it.

It sounds contradictory to say that something is both "natural" and a "technique," but that's how it works: Nature is an orderly thing, and anything orderly is technical or "techniquable." Walking is a "technique" for getting from one place to another, so to speak, and it's at the same time "natural." A child learning to walk perceives it as a technical problem, that is, until he learns how, then he sees it as being natural. Meditation is the same way, it's perfectly natural but *seems* contrived in the beginning. Once you learn to meditate, however, it becomes as natural as walking, and you can maintain the meditative state without thinking about it, "doing" it or "practicing" it.

The meditative state and the objective state are one and the same state. We refer to them by different names depending on when they are being "practiced": When in daily activity, we call it *being objective*; when we practice it in a formal, structured, concentrated setting, we call it *meditation*.

Balancing Activity With Receptivity

Meditation balances movement with rest. To be active and outgoing without balancing it with periods of stillness and receptivity is to live one-sidely. And one-sidedness or extremism in anything marks the immature, emotional person. In order to be effective and creative, activity *must* be balanced by receptivity.

Meditation *is* receptivity; it's just sitting still and listening with alertness. It's inactivity, but the inaction isn't dead; it's very dynamic. You're not "doing" anything, not using effort or will power, yet you are accomplishing everything -

you are accomplishing balance, which is the universal will, direction, goal, and law.

In activity your movement is outward, away from yourself and toward the situation or toward the other person; in meditation, on the other hand, the movement is inward, toward yourself, toward your heart, soul, or center. In activity you are an extrovert; in meditation, you balance it by being an introvert, by looking inward. During our school years, we cultivate an outgoing personality to increase our sociability. But extroversion at this stage is relatively shallow because it's not balanced by looking within. Unless we learn how to look within, we cannot grow beyond the "nice" personality stage but will remain stunted in mediocrity.

A person cannot be an intelligent and authentic extrovert without first looking within, for in order to know another, one must first know one's self. I can't see who you are until I see who I am. I can't relate and communicate with you (the world) until I relate and communicate with myself.

The Meditation Exercise

Meditation is the relaxation of the mind through closely observing its activity from a distance. The only problem is, we're not used to being relaxed and are easily distracted. We can't concentrate for more than a few seconds without being carried away or lost in our thoughts. So we need something to fix our attention on, some object that will serve as an anchor to prevent our attention from wandering.

The object we'll use here will be our *breathing*, but it can be anything: it can be staring at a lighted candle, a spot on the wall, a flower, or a picture of a beloved or special person; it can be repetitive praying with the aid of rosary beads, the chanting of some mantra, syllable or positive affirmation, or the concentrating on an imaginary symbol or on the movement of one's naval, and so on, depending on your cultural background, personality, or state of mind. We will use a "breathing meditation" because it is a natural and powerful one, one that has been practiced and proven over thousands of years by people of all the major religions and philosophies, and one that is compatible with the busy life-style of the computer-age American.

Formal meditation practice consists of three main elements: (1) focusing attention between your eyebrows: (2) following your breathing; and (3) noticing when thoughts distract you from following your breathing. That's all there is to it. Let's now look at the details.

Meditation should be practiced twice-daily, preferably at a regular time and place, and for periods of about fifteen minutes each. The best time is as soon as possible after waking, and then again about twelve hours later. It's better before eating than after. A full stomach decreases sensitivity because the digestive process uses a lot of energy.

Attitude

The right attitude is crucial to success in meditation. By right attitude I mean that meditation shouldn't be regarded casually but considered as important and necessary as proper exercise, nutrition, and sleep. Or rather, it should be considered more important than these things, for unless you are in the right frame of mind, you won't exercise, eat properly, or sleep very well. The quality of every aspect of your life depends on the tranquillity of your mind; therefore, make the twice-daily practice of meditation the top priority. Let it be the foundation of your day, the foundation of your life. Let meditation be the center around which all other activities revolve.

Preparation

Sit in a chair with your back and neck as straight as possible, but not to the point of discomfort. This facilitates breathing and the flow of energy and information which must travel up the spine to reach the brain. Feet should be flat and hands should be touching to help concentrate energy and prevent it from escaping. Close your eyes and mouth, and breathe normally through your nose. Scan your body to locate and relax any physical tension. Put aside all family, business, and personal concerns. There is a time for everything, and this is the time for the luxury and necessity of total freedom, peace, and solitude.

Focusing Attention Between The Eyebrows

Begin by focusing your attention slightly upwards between the eyebrows and holding it there as still as possible. This is the area of the brain where thoughts surface from the subconscious, where they first dawn into awareness. When we're straining to think of something, we instinctively look up toward this area. By fixing your attention here, like a cat at a mouse-hole, you can catch and observe thoughts at the very point of their arising. This "being present at the inception of thought" is the heart and essence of meditation; this is called being "centered" or "poised," and is the state you want to carry with you throughout the day.

Following Your Breathing

Now at the same time your attention is focused there, be *very* aware of your breathing moving in and then out, in and then out. As you are watching your breathing, resist the natural tendency to move your attention down toward the nostrils, but remain *firmly* focused between the eyebrows. You want to breathe as if through your forehead. It will get easier with practice. Breathe as naturally as possible. Try not to effect it or control it any way; just flow along with it as it is. Don't go ahead of it or lag behind it; just be simultaneous with it, in unison with it. Join it as it comes in, curls around, and goes out; in, around, and out.

Noticing Distracting Thoughts

Whenever you notice your mind has wandered off, gently return attention to your breathing again and again. Each time a random thought arises, notice it has, then come back to being very aware of your breathing again. Do not become annoyed or impatient with yourself for taking so long to notice these thoughts. With practice, you will become more and more alert and responsive. Remember, meditation has no goal or object; it's not a competitive activity. You cannot win at it or lose at it; it's an end in and of itself. There are benefits, of course, but we don't do it for the benefits; we do it because that's how being conscious works; that's *how* to be conscious. Meditation is the act of being aware. That's all we're doing when we meditate - just being fully aware in and of the present moment.

Meditation isn't hypnosis; it's just the opposite - it frees us from hypnosis. We're hypnotized right now in the sense that we're under the influence of our past conditioning, training, environment, and emotions. We're hypnotized in the sense that we're unwittingly susceptible to outside influences instead of our own. The hypnotized person doesn't know he's hypnotized. He thinks he's himself. My friend Maxie Pierpont was put in a trance by a stage hypnotist and told to walk around in his underwear. As Maxie returned to his seat without his pants on, the audience roared with laughter. Maxie didn't know why they were laughing. He thought it must've been something he said on stage while under hypnosis. He had no idea he was *still* under it. He knew he had no pants on but *didn't think anything of it.* It was not until the hypnotist snapped his fingers to break the trance that Maxie realized the truth. We're all walking around in our underwear in the sense that we're being manipulated either by the past, or by someone else's idea of what we should be, do, have, and believe. As the hypnotist snapped his fingers to return Maxie to reality, so meditation works to snap us back to reality. It returns us back to ourselves, back to our original state of calmness, clarity and contentment.

Meditation itself is not concentration either, in the true sense of the word. True concentration implies effort or force which is tiring and energy-draining. In meditation, we are being alert, paying one-pointed attention, but there isn't or shouldn't be any exertion involved. We are merely focusing our attention in a particular direction rather than having it inefficiently scattered. This will, of course, take some getting used to, and this is where the effort comes in. Meditation, consciousness, existence itself, is effortless; it's getting there that takes effort.

Meditation may be more accurately called a *discipline* than a concentration exercise. Learning to meditate, like learning anything new, will take time, resolution, and perseverance. Everything is difficult in the beginning and meditation is no exception. Meditation is both a technique and the state that technique would bring you to. The technique itself can be learned in a few minutes, but the meditative state is what has to be discovered on your own through disciplined practice. This may take a few days or weeks. The experience itself is simply a feeling of heightened awareness and deep tranquillity, although your response in the beginning might be something like, "ooh, I seee!" or "aahaaa!"

The simple "watching" of thought,as we've been discussing, is the whole kcy to controlling it. We can't stop the mind by effort, force, or willpower, but when we just watch it from a distance - it stops.

We are not concerned with *what* the mind thinks; our only concern is to closely watch it *whatever* and *whenever* it thinks. The idea is to be perfectly still in order to discern the slightest movement as an animal does when it senses something amiss. Notice when thoughts arise and then let them go; dissolve them. Hold your awareness in advance of thought. Anticipate their coming. Be ready for them. And when they come, just let them evaporate in the energy of your awareness. You don't want to be blank or closed, that's not the idea; the idea is to stay openly aware of anything that distracts you away from watching your breathing, whether it's a sound, smell, itch, thought or feeling, and then return attention to your breathing again and again.

The mind is a genetic hand-me-down from the past, and to be controlled by it would mean being controlled by the past. If we were controlled by the past, there could be no growth; there could be nothing new, no creativity but only a long drawn-out boring stagnation. If our genes and environment were the sole determinants of our activity, then we would be no different than animals, but we are of a different and higher order than animals in more than just an evolutionary sense. Animals are led only by their stomachs and genitals, but we have a higher leading; we are led by the spirit - the spirit of love and intelligence - the spirit of what is true, right, and good. Meditation puts the body and spirit back into their balanced and proper relationship; that is, with the spirit leading and the body/mind following, and both working together as one.

Three Types Of Mental Activity

During meditation you will encounter three general types of mental activity. The first and most common type is *daydreaming*. Daydreaming is when the mind is not directed and just wanders off on its own. One thought reminds you of another which triggers another, and so on. It's engaging in idle reverie, fantasy, nostalgia; it's thinking of a hope or a wish being fulfilled; it's thinking of last night's conversation, etc. This is not meditation, so as often as you catch yourself doing it, return to observing your breathing through the bottom of your forehead.

We can refer to the second type of mental activity as *contemplation*, which is just another word for thinking or deliberating. Contemplation is the weighing or studying of some issue; it is creative brainstorming or attempting to solve some personal or business problem, etc. Contemplation is in a higher class than daydreaming because it's more directed and productive and is done more consciously, but it's in a lower class than "insight" which is *knowledge without thinking at all*. So whenever you find yourself contemplating instead of meditating, patiently return attention to your breathing again and again.

Insight is the third type of thing you'll experience during the practice of meditation. Insight is not "mental activity" in the sense the above two cases are; it's an experience of knowing, of direct and immediate knowing without the intervention of thought. Insights are elucidating glimpses of reality; they are seeing into the true nature of some aspect of yourself or the world. They may be quite profound and frequent during the first few weeks or months of meditation; thereafter, they become increasingly subtle. Some insights may be beautiful beyond words, and you may laugh or cry with joy. And some may be painful as real or imagined events and fears from the past spring up from the subconscious mind to be seen clearly and completely for the first time. Here, too, you may laugh or cry with joy - the joy of relief, for as these emotions bubble up, purge, and dissipate before your eyes, so does all the tension that went with them. As a result, you will feel cleansed, purified, light, refreshed, relaxed, changed, born again, renewed.

Meditation does for accumulated tension what dreams do for daily tension. One purpose of dreams is to relax any emotional tension that may have built up during the day, so we'll wake up refreshed mentally as well as physically.

Dreams stimulate emotional release in the same way movies do: a tragic story releases tears; a comedy releases laughter. When the hero finally frees himself from his dangerous predicament, some of our own fear is relaxed as well. While the drama in movies, books and dreams provides some relief of superficial tension, it's not powerful enough to break up the tension accumulated from childhood. For this we need to meditate. Meditation is both a means by which repressed tension may surface and dissolve, and a state of mind by which it cannot return.

When an experience of insight or revelation occurs, however major or minor, just experience it fully and indifferently and then return to your breathing again. (In cases where, for example, some original idea occurs to you, or the solution to some problem presents itself, you may want to interrupt the meditation and write it down so as not to forget it or be distracted by it. But be careful not to use meditation as a brainstorming session - brainstorm some other time.)

Now insight and intelligence are one and the same thing, and are the chief benefits of meditation (along with health and happiness), but the only way to cultivate it is to be indifferent to it. We don't want to be insightful or intelligent just for a moment here and there; we want to be intelligent always. And the way to be so is to be detached and indifferent always. Experience an insight to the fullest, but don't get carried away by it in the slightest. In this way, moments of insight will progressively widen from a split second in duration, to a minute, to an hour, to a day, to all the time.

Some Effects And Benefits

Except for being more relaxed and aware, you will usually come out of these meditation sessions feeling no different than when you began. In general, your meditation periods will be uneventful, and it will *seem* as though nothing positive or effective is happening. But meditation works in very subtle ways. The quality of your life will almost immediately improve, but you may not connect it to meditation because it will all be perfectly natural. For instance, you'll find yourself working smarter instead of harder; your sense of humor and sense of proportion will improve; you'll tend to be more affectionate and communicative with loved ones, and more tolerant, patient, and compassionate in general.

You'll become more discriminating as to the quality and value of things. You'll be able to discern more readily between good and bad friends, advisors, food, books, art, music, conversation, business opportunities, etc.

Your appearance will quickly improve: The skin on your face will tighten-up as vitality and alertness return to it, and you will tend to stand up straighter, with your shoulders back, and your chest out.

Your general health will improve as meditation can help to control, reverse, or prevent such stress-related symptoms as insomnia, high blood pressure, headaches, lower back pain, ulcers, compulsive overeating, some kinds of cancer, infertility, arthritis, menstrual discomfort, allergies, skin disease, heart disease (to name just a few), as well as dependence on tranquillizers, alcohol, marijuana, nicotine, caffeine, cocaine, sugar, etc.

How is meditation able to do this? The first thing to understand is that all these diseases are *symptoms* or *effects* of an underlying problem. That underlying problem is tension, stress, uneasiness. The root meaning of the word *disease* is "reversal of ease" or "dis-ease." Stress-related disease, then, begins in the mind, and if not checked, spreads to the body. It moves from the mental to the physical, beginning as a tiny germ and growing to debilitating proportions. So heart disease, etc., is not the *real* problem; the real problem is stress - mistakenly taking life personally, egotistically, emotionally. Heart disease is merely the manifestation, the symptom, the effect. Tension is the cause, heart disease, smoking, etc., are the effects. So to reverse these diseases, we simply have to reverse the tension, and that's what meditation does - it returns you to your natural and original state of easiness.

But as it took a while for your body to become infected, it will take a while for it to recover after you've become relaxed - that is, you may not stop smoking or drinking immediately even though your mind is at ease because your *body* is still contaminated and will need some time to detoxify. And likewise with an ulcer or heart disease, etc.; the physical healing may lag behind the mental or emotional healing.

Which one of these diseases tension will cause is determined by heredity and the environment. If we have a family history of ulcers, cancer, diabetes, alcoholism, etc. that's what we'll be predisposed to getting. It doesn't mean we *will* get it; it means that if we continually violate the law of balance - we will. Of course, we all have to die of something sooner or later; the idea is to make it later than sooner.

Now the medical doctor is trained only to deal with *effects*, not with causes. His job is to diagnose and treat only the *symptoms* of the disease, not the disease itself. Consequently, a patient's heart disease will either return after being treated, or the stress will express itself in some other part of the body later on. True healing involves eliminating the *cause*, and only *you* can do that. The doctor can reduce the inflammation, but only you can eliminate the fuel that feeds it.

The most active ingredient in a doctor's intervention is his ability to bring you to relax. The doctor can give the patient a placebo, for example, and the most terrible disease can reverse. Why? Because the patient *believed* the "medicine" would work, relaxed, and it did! Thus, the patient really healed himself. He believed he could be healed, relaxed, and was healed. Albert Schweitzer said, "All healing is self-healing." The doctor's medicines and "bedside manner" serve merely to compensate for the patient's inability to relax, his inability to get out of the way and let the healing forces of nature run their course.

When you step on a nail, all the forces of nature rush to the scene to make repairs: a pain chemical is released to inform the brain that a "false" object is sticking in your foot and to please remove it as soon as possible; at the same time, other agents come to eject the nail, disinfect the area, stop the bleeding, and begin grafting the torn skin back together.

Emotional pain also indicates that something is wrong, that some foreign, false, or negative thought has invaded the mind. Now just as the first step in physical healing is to remove the nail, the first step in emotional healing is to remove (control) the negative thought or feeling. As the nail is "false" to the body, so negative thoughts and their accompanying tension are false to the mind. The nail is real in the sense that it's certainly sticking in your foot and certainly hurts, but is false in the sense that it doesn't belong there, it isn't natural. Likewise, negative thoughts and tension are real in the sense that they do exist, but are false in that they don't belong there; they don't occur in nature; they are artificial.

Staying Alert

Objectivity or relaxation can come by degree, or it can come all at once. You can gradually become relaxed over a period of weeks, months, or years; or, in a single, spontaneous let-go, decades of residual tension can be wiped out in a second. The instant route is, of course, more appealing, but unfortunately, spontaneity cannot be premeditated; it's an obvious contradiction. You'll either become spontaneously relaxed or you won't, but you can't plan it. What you *can* do, however, is stay ready and receptive so that, in the first place, it *can* come, and in the second place, when it does, *you will be there*. The nature of spontaneity is to delight by surprise, but if you are never home, or the doors and windows of your mind are closed, you'll keep missing and missing. It's a situation similar to that of a door-to-door salesman who needs only one sale per day to earn a living, but in order to make that one sale, he must knock on a hundred doors. And just as the salesman cannot know in advance which house contains the buyer, you cannot know at which moment relaxation will come, but must remain ready, alert, and receptive at *every* moment.

CHAPTER 9

BEING PRESENT

*The **P**resent is the **O**nly **I**nstant **S**ecurity can be **E**xperienced*

The future hasn't occurred yet, so is always a part of the imagination; the past is history, so is always a part of the memory. The only reality there is, then, is the *present moment.*

The present moment is the point of calmness, contentment, and clarity. Only here and now can the mind be still, satisfied, and aware. The still mind doesn't move to the past or to the future, the satisfied mind doesn't desire to, and the aware mind knows that the past and future are departures from reality.

Being in the present means to be *totally* involved in the thing you are doing *right now*. It means your attention is not divided between this moment and what happened earlier or what you will do later. When you are eating, showering, dressing or driving, for instance, notice that your mind is not on those things, but is elsewhere. And if you trace your activities through the whole day, you'll see that your mind is almost never on the thing at hand, but on something in the past or future. This is called not living in the present moment, and is equal to the imbalanced state of mind.

We "think" we're intelligent because our mind is working on several things at a time, or is several steps ahead of what's happening. But the reverse is true - not staying rooted in the present moment makes us dull: we don't know what a shower feels like; we don't know what food tastes like; we don't remember people's names, what we just read, what we had for breakfast, and so on. We're like drunks who always make it home, but never know how we did it.

The Present Is The Point Of Security

To be effective and secure, one doesn't have to refer to the past or look forward to the future, for both are already inherent in the present. The present is a self-contained universe that doesn't require anything external to it. Anything from the past that would somehow be useful and relevant to this moment will spontaneously be available to you. You don't have to "remember" that a stove might be hot, or to look both ways before crossing - you just have to be alert in the present moment. Living in the present doesn't mean you are not careful or do not pause before an important decision; it means you pause and use caution spontaneously.

If a person is alert in the present, the future will take care of itself, but if not, nothing from the past will help him. By living according to the past he may not repeat the *same* mistake again, but he will make different ones all the time which is just as bad. He will find himself always "chalking things up to experience," doing and saying the wrong things at the wrong time, not being quite "with it," "right there" or "right on." Reality is going on, but he will be constantly out of sync with it, constantly lagging a little bit behind it because he must always refer to his memory before he can respond. Even if it takes only a split-second, it's too late; the moment has passed; the boat has been missed. Life is happening *now* and must be responded to *now*. To always miss it by only a split-second is still to always miss it.

The average person erroneously "believes" that by not being tethered to the past, he would be as if lost in deep space without any point of reference. He feels the need for something to hang on to. So for the sake of security, he wants every person, situation, and moment to be a carbon copy of every other. He wants to know everything he will say and do *in advance*. He is uncomfortable in novel situations and with people of different backgrounds and cultures because they will require original and unrehearsed responses.

So the person living from the past instead of the present sacrifices spontaneity and originality (which is life itself) for a false sense of security. False because he is no more secure than an ostrich hiding its head in the sand. Responding to life fully, correctly, and confidently is based primarily on knowing what's happening *right now*, and the only way to know, is to *be there* right now. The experience of the past is a secondary and inferior consideration. The past is academic; the present is real life being lived in real time. It is whole and complete so is free of error and apprehension.

The Present Is The Point Of Control

Living from the past is like joining a conversation already in progress; living in the present is like being the person who initiated the conversation. The person in the latter case feels, of course, much more secure that the one in the former. The person joining the group late will not feel completely at ease because he doesn't yet know the topic under discussion or the mood of the group. Until he does, he is not really present, not really a participant, but a spectator, a bystander. The person who first sparked the conversation is the most powerful and secure because he was present at the very beginning so was privy to every aspect of its development. He's the most powerful because he's the most knowledgeable, and the most knowledgeable because, the most present.

By virtue of his being fully present at each moment of the discussion, he will, in effect, control it. He will be aware when the talk is straying off course and will be the one to steer it back. Or if the subject deserves to be strayed from, he will be the one to subtly initiate the change. To control doesn't mean to dominate; it means to be aware of the purpose of a thing and to be creative in achieving that purpose. To participate fully means to participate creatively. The purpose and objective of the conversation, in the example I'm using here, is purely social; i.e., to meet new people, to share ideas, information and interests. The person who is most present is simply the one who most consciously facilitates this purpose.

He is effective because to be present means to be ego-less or self-less, and without a self to satisfy or defend, he can participate with his whole being. He doesn't need to hold anything back, but is free to commit 100 percent of himself to the issue at hand.

The mind, the ego, cannot exist in the present moment; it's a contradiction. The nature of the ego, because it is false, is to constantly move with fear, nervousness, doubt, defensiveness. But in the present, because the present is real, there is only stillness, a stillness that translates to honesty, strength, and confidence.

To Be Present Is To Be Still

"Conscious reality" can be defined as: *the present moment integration of physical movement with mental stillness.* It is the marriage of body and soul. All physical activity, everything we do such as talking, listening, working, happens in the present, and in order for the mind to be in tune with what's happening, it must be flexible. To be still, relaxed, is to be flexible. The more still the mind, the more flexible, and the more flexible, the more adaptable to lightning-fast, moment-to-moment activity. In order for consciousness to keep up with this activity, that is to say, in order to be conscious of reality, the mind must move at the exact same speed as reality, and, paradoxically, the only way it can do that is to remain perfectly still.

The present is equal to the meditation state where your attention is focused at the very intersection of consciousness in order to notice the slightest movement. Mental stillness and presence of mind are one and the same state. As soon as the mind leaves stillness to become emotional - you have left the present moment as well. The rule of thumb is this: If your mind is still, you are "here"; if it's going, you are "gone." To regain the moment, simply be indifferently aware of your thoughts until they subside, just as you would during meditation.

The present moment and the tension-free state of balance are the same thing. The present is like neutral gear in an automobile, the position in which there's no stress on the engine, and the position in which the car is now poised to move in any direction at any time. The future and past are like the forward and reverse gears; they are the positions of movement or emotion. In the forward position you can't go backwards; and in the reverse position you can't go forward. So you are not only stressed, but are limited to only one position at a time. To choose one position is to sacrifice the other. In any given moment, half of your possibilities are denied. But in reality, in the present moment, you can move in neutral, forward, and reverse, all at the same time.

How can that be? Because emotional movement and creative movement work in different directions: emotion moves horizontally; creativity moves vertically. Emotional movement, which is in error, moves forward or backward, to the future or to the past; but creative movement is inward and outward. By moving inwardly and expressing it outwardly, you are not only able to travel in "neutral" and without stress, but can travel in both forward and reverse at the exact same time as well - for as you move, you pull the entire past and entire future along with you simultaneously! When you move in the right direction, the whole ball of wax, the whole universe, all knowledge, moves with you.

Balancing Method With Madness

To the degree we are present, we possess total knowledge; to the degree we are not, we possess partial knowledge. And because life is a circular phenomenon there's no end to knowledge and no end to the present moment. We can penetrate it infinitely, and it will be new, different, and full of wonder infinitely. The paradoxical universe is in a state of endless flux where each moment is totally unrelated to any that has passed or any that is to come. It's in perfect order and perfect chaos at the same time. It's chaotic in an orderly way - like a dancer. The dancer is moving chaotically, freely, but is at the same time in step with the beat. The dancer is as if mad, but there's a method to her madness. To the biased person who can see but not hear, the dancer looks crazy; but to the balanced person who can hear the music as well as see the movements - it all makes sense.

In practical terms, this explains why successful living requires that you break with the past, that you totally disconnect yourself from all that you've thought and done before. Success doesn't come by moving in orderly, calculated steps alone, as the textbooks teach, but also by moving in quantum leaps as the universe teaches. In other words, you don't have to work your way up from clerk to president in sequential order, you can come in the front door as already the president. The difference between the clerk and the president is their state of mind, their attitude. Both may be equally qualified, the only difference is - one knows it, the other doesn't. The masses cling to the apron strings of the past. They'll do nothing unless it's been done before - but then it's too late - nobody wants it. Success demands a leap of faith, a jump into the unknown, a jump into the abyss of the present moment. It's to forget everything you've ever been taught and told and to immediately be that which you already are.

Living With A Passion

Let's assume that we're either not in the present moment at all, or we are to a low degree. Let's assume that in any given moment most of our attention is directed either toward the past or toward some future event or result, so that very little energy remains to experience what is happening right here and now. For instance, if you are reading these words and at the same time are trying to correlate them with what you already know, or if you are underlining some passages with a view toward re-reading them at future time, then you are not in the present moment, so will miss the whole book. By programming your subconscious with the idea that you will re-read the book at a later time, you effectively excuse yourself from having to pay attention right now. If you've invested money and time in a book, but not the energy, then it's all for nothing. The way to read a book is to assume it's the last copy in existance and that after you read it, it too will be destroyed. Then you will drink every word. You will read it with the same passion and energy with which it was written. Now, instead of seeing the words superficially, you will be able to read between the lines and see different levels of meaning. And what is meaningful or useful to you will simply stay with you, and what is not, will not.

But if you try to come back to a book at a later time, it won't be the same; it will be like a stranger. In the first place, you will be in a different mood, a different frame of mind. You won't be the same person you were then. The state of mind that prompts you to read a particular book at a particular time can't be duplicated. The book and the state of mind are a marriage, a matched set. They come and go together. They are inseparable and irreplaceable. And in the second place, if you weren't present the first time around, you won't be present the second time either.

Every aspect of life is to be treated with this same now-is-the-only-time- there-is attitude. All energy must be concentrated in the present moment whatever the activity, otherwise its meaning and value will be missed. You are here and now. Time, money, and effort has been spent to bring you to this moment. Are you now going to waste it by denying it your total and undivided attention? To live passionately is to assume that all past moments have been destroyed and the only one we have to go by is this one. And since this moment is an ongoing, infinite, circular continuum, it's all that is ever necessary; it is enough. If we digest this moment completely, then the next one will be the richer for it, but if we skim this moment, the next will be the poorer, so that even if we were to read a thousand books and live a thousand years, we'd be just as dull as ever.

The moment at hand is the entrance to life, the entrance to truth - its blood is to be drunk and its flesh is to be eaten. Our task is to enter this moment and to never leave it and to realize that there's no end to it. When Robin Hood's antagonist hit the bull's-eye, everyone believed the game was over and began to leave. But Robin Hood didn't believe it - and proceeded to split the arrow. This moment is like the arrow at the center of the bull's-eye - it can be split indefinitely. To the degree you remain in the center of the moment, there's no end to the game; to the degree you look forward or backward, the game's over.

The idea is to experience this moment so completely that nothing of it is left over to carry around in your memory banks. We want to enter the moment cleanly and leave it cleanly. We want to end the moment when the moment is ended, not leave it with unresolved questions or with hangovers of resentment, doubt, regret, guilt. Let what comes up in the moment also go down with it. Have no unfinished business. Find your house clean and leave it clean. Settle an issue on the spot. If a bully isn't stood up to there and then, he will trouble you always. Make all your actions complete and total. A sharpshooter doesn't aim and *then* fire - he aims and fires simultaneously. There's no space between the aiming and the firing; it's a single, unified action. Let the moment be the same way - single, unified, all-inclusive; let it come out of itself and return to itself. Penetrate each moment with calmness and contentment and leave it the same way; that is, without accumulating anything in the process, such as the desire that the next moment be the same or different.

To the degree you remain in the present, all the knowledge necessary to attaining your moment-to-moment and long term goals will be spontaneously available to you. You are being constantly guided by an inner sense or spirit of wholeness. This spirit is what tells you what course of action to take in various circumstances, what to say and not to say, what to do and when to do it, etc. This harmonizing spirit wants you and your goals to become one happy whole. In the present moment you become receptive to its direction. You become guided from within. consequently, all you'll have to do is open your mouth and only what's positive and appropriate will come out.

You will never have to worry about saying or doing the wrong thing, because in the present moment you will be spontaneous love, and love can do no wrong. The person who is not in the moment cannot love spontaneously. He discriminates between who he will be sensitive to or not based on his biases or self-interest. He is considerate only to the degree he perceives you to be substantial in some way. If you stop him to ask directions to a particular street, he will look over your car before responding. If it's a new car, he will give you long, careful, detailed instructions; if it's an older car, he will just point. The person without love lives in fear that he might accidentally be rude to a bank president, or worse, that he might accidentally be respectful to the dishwasher. But the person who lives in the present moment is fearless and confident because he loves without discrimination. He enters the moment established in love so needs not be concerned with who you are or how to act. He is love and you are equal to it. No other knowledge is necessary. Thus he lives without error or effort.

Seizing The Moment

The present is elusive and precarious; once you've found it, you must hang onto it like a surfer riding the crest of a wave. The crest is his "moment"; once he's found it, he can't let it go. While riding it, he's in heaven and the very picture of grace and beauty. But if he loses it - into the drink he flops.

Or it's like a rodeo cowboy riding a bucking bronco: being seated on the bull when the bell rings and the gate flies open is his "moment." As long as he and the bull move as one animal, all is well; nothing can happen to him. But as soon as a little time or space develops between the bull's back and the cowboy's bottom-that's the end of the cowboy.

The present requires a total commitment. It can't be entered into half-heartedly or with shyness or apprehension. The present can't be entered into just a little bit. One is either alive or dead; there's no in-between. To be only half alive is like a tire with a slow leak. It functions, but has no future, no potential. It has nothing to look forward to but to go flat; nothing to look forward to but death. Life is slowly leaking away and there is no hope. For the man who is half alive, half conscious, life is a dreadful, hopeless situation.

But he is mistaken - there *is* hope; there *is* something else. The egotistical, intellectual, conventional man thinks he knows all there is to know. He thinks that if he doesn't know a thing then it must be unknowable. But he is wrong. Why? Because 85 percent of his potential knowledge has yet to be tapped and experienced and he cannot possibly know what it contains. The "something else" that's missing from his life is contained within that 85 percent, but unless he's fully present, he will never realize it. Once he does realize it, however, then he's free; then he can not only live in peace, but die in peace. Once a person has experienced the joy or the understanding that comes with being fully conscious of life, even if only for a second - then he can die in peace; he will be ready. It's as if he's been given 75 years solely for the purpose of finding that one moment, and once he's found it he would gladly have traded his whole life for it - for 75 years of false living is no match for a single moment of truth.

Being Already Dead

Just as dying before one is ready is among the most tragic things, so being ready to die is among the most beautiful. And the way to be ready to die is to *assume you are dead already*. Accept the fact that you're already dead, and that this moment is just a fluke, just a miracle, just an oversight on the part of existance. You're going to be dead in a few years anyway, why not be egotistically dead right now? What real difference will another 2 or 3 or 5 or 10 years make? What are you going to do then that you haven't done up till now? Visit Niagara Falls? Niagara Falls isn't going to make you free. First become free, *then* go places and do things, because only then will your eyes be open to appreciate them. And the way to be free is to die to the present moment, to risk your whole life in it, to put all your trust in it. Before there can be the new, the old must be discarded; before you can awaken, the past must be put to sleep. Being reserved and prudent is appropriate in business and social affairs, but life, consciousness, and happiness demand that nothing be held back; commitment must be total and absolute. There can be no looking back, no hesitation, for this moment is all there is, all there ever has been, and all there ever will be. Within it is realized the whole theme of life - to relax and enjoy and to love without inhibition.